D1165905

The MONOCLE
Travel Guide Series

Toronto

For more information,
please visit *gestalten.com*

———

Bibliographic information
published by the Deutsche
Nationalbibliothek: The Deutsche
Nationalbibliothek lists this publi-
cation in the Deutsche National-
bibliografie; detailed bibliographic
data are available online
at *dnb.d-nb.de*

Monocle editor in chief:
Tyler Brûlé
Monocle editor: *Andrew Tuck*
Books editor: *Joe Pickard*
Guide editors: *Tomos Lewis, Jason Li*

———

Designed by *Monocle*
Proofreading by *Monocle*
Typeset in *Plantin & Helvetica*

———

Printed by *Offsetdruckerei
Grammlich, Pliezhausen*

Made in Germany

Published by *Gestalten,* Berlin 2016
ISBN 978-3-89955-683-4

© Die Gestalten Verlag GmbH &
Co. KG, Berlin 2016

This book was printed on
paper certified by the FSC®

Welcome
—— A city evolving

Toronto is akin to a teenager: energetic, fickle and unwieldy at times. But while Canada's largest city may occasionally suffer from the odd growing pain, it's continually transforming in beguiling ways.

Since its founding on the edge of magnificent *Lake Ontario* in 1834, waves of immigrants from around the world have flocked here, attracted by the city's tolerant nature and creative outlook; today, more than half of its 2.8 million residents were born elsewhere. This *diversity* reveals itself in one of the most thrilling mixes of vibrant restaurants, boutique hotels, cocktail bars, *independent clothing shops* and design studios to be found anywhere in the country.

MONOCLE has had a bureau in Toronto since 2012; it's a city that we're deeply passionate about. For this guide the editorial team dug deep to uncover the *lesser-known architectural gems*, the most innovative art galleries and intriguing and historic neighbourhoods in which to wander. We also provide plenty of advice on making the most of Ontario's climactic extremes – whether that's a toasty bar in which to hole up in on a cold day, *a winter sport* to try your hand at or the most handsome park, *restaurant terrace* or outdoor swimming pool in which to soak up that precious summer sun.

Toronto is changing, and changing fast. Delve into the pages that follow to discover one of North America's most intriguing urban hubs for yourself. — (M)

Contents
—— Navigating the city

Use the key below to help navigate the guide section by section.

012 —— 013
Map
Take stock of Toronto with our handy map of the city, helping you get to grips with the key areas covered in this guide.

014 —— 015
Need to know
From politics to hockey, tipping to apologising, here are some of the basics for navigating the city's streets, sights and citizens.

016 —— 025
Hotels
There's no shortage of options when it comes to accommodation in Toronto, from boutique hotels in former punk bars right up to purpose-built luxury high rises. Find out where to stay for business or pleasure with our guide to the best hotels.

026 —— 047
Food and drink
A multicultural population gives a city a multicultural menu, and Toronto has one of the most varied on Earth. Whether you're drawn to Canadian staples, Asian or even African, you're in the right place to fill your boots.

048 —— 069
Retail
Toronto is a city where small businesses thrive and independent retailers are treasured. So hit the streets with our guide to the best in fashion, homeware, concept shops and everything in between.

070 —— 072
Things we'd buy
Here's our pick of Toronto's take-homes, from Mountie-themed flasks to coffee and craft beer.

073 —— 096
Essays
Toronto is diverse in population, outlook and personalities, so it can be a challenge to grasp its measure. Here, Monocle family and friends uncover various elements of the city to show you what life here is really like.

Map
—— The city at a glance

The city of Toronto covers more than 640 sq km on a wide plain north of Lake Ontario, its central area carved into three by the Don River in the east and the Humber to the west.

Given that diversity is a particular point of pride to Torontonians it shouldn't be much of a surprise to learn that there are some 140 neighbourhoods in the city, each with an individual character. So while the majority of the attractions can be found in the fast-paced Downtown area (bordered by the lake to the south, the Don River to the east, Bloor Street to the north and Bathurst Street to the west), striking out a little further afield certainly pays dividends.

Crossing the Don will take you to Leslieville, with its old-meets-new appeal, and only a little way north are well-to-do Summerhill and Rosedale and a heartland of 19th-century residences. Or, for a more laidback village vibe, head for Roncesvalles, west past the city's treasured Trinity Bellwoods Park.

Summerhill

Evergreen
Brick Works

l Ontario
useum

COVERY
TRICT

CHURCH AND
WELLESLEY

CABBAGETOWN

Don River

REGENT PARK

Guild Park

BALDWIN
VILLAGE

YONGE-DUNDAS

Dundas Street

Yonge Street

University Avenue

CORKTOWN

Leslieville

Gallery of Ontario
• OCAD Building

• Massey Hall

OLD TOWN

ATOWN

Toronto City Hall

DISTILLERY DISTRICT

EEN STREET
WEST

FINANCIAL
DISTRICT

Princess of
es Theatre
ll Lightbox •

Roy Thomson
Hall

• Toronto-Dominion
Centre
Fairmont Royal • Sony Centre
• York Hotel   for the Performing Arts

St Lawrence
Market

TERTAINMENT
DISTRICT

Toronto Union Station

Air Canada Centre

CN Tower

HARBOURFRONT

The Power Plant
Contemporary Art Gallery

INNER HARBOUR

ly Bishop
o City Airport

oronto Islands

0   500m   N

Need to know
—— Get to grips with the basics

Whether it's where to take shelter on a bitter winter's day, how to navigate your way around an ice hockey game or how much to tip your waiter for that round of Caesars (cocktails) you've just bought, the following will guide you through the essentials for your visit to Canada's largest city.

Making money
Currency

In 2011, Canada switched its currency from paper to polymer bills. They are impossible to counterfeit, durable, environmentally friendly and feature prominent Canadian personalities and inventions, such as the so-called "Canada arm" designed for the International Space Station. The one and two-dollar coins are named after the national bird, the Arctic loon. One dollar is a "loonie"; a two-dollar coin is (imaginatively) a "toonie".

Where do we begin?
Origins

The name Toronto derives from a Mohawk word – *tkaronto* – roughly meaning "where there are trees standing in the water". The submerged woodland may have long gone but the legacy of the Laurentide Ice Sheet, which receded about 12,500 years ago, is still clear. Toronto is a city of ravines, scars of the ice age. The fertile land supported settlers of what would become Canada's largest city, formally founded by the British in 1834. Today downtown Toronto is home to 2.7 million people.

Hurry up, Papachan. I can't hold this pose for long

And look, that's where they grow all those cabbages...

Village people
Neighbourhoods

Maps of Toronto can be a little deceptive: the city is a patchwork of former villages and towns woven into an urban sprawl. The result is a "city of neighbourhoods" but while there are 140 of these officially, in practice there are hundreds more. Torontonians often refer to streets as districts and have a penchant for colloquial names, although sometimes these morph into "formal" mantles over the years; Cabbagetown is a prime example.

Get your skates on
Ice hockey

Few things bring Canadians together quite like ice hockey. Its players are national treasures, victories become part of the country's psyche and defeats can (occasionally) lead to rioting in the streets. The regular season runs from October to April (the Stanley Cup contest is between April and June) and "Hockey Night in Canada" broadcasts are still among the most-watched televised events of the year.

The party's over
City politics

Torontonians often feel more engaged with the politics of their city than their nation. Canada's largest city operates a "weak mayor/strong council" system, which means the figurehead of political life cannot rule by decree. Toronto's late former mayor Rob Ford challenged this model, however. City hall's members do carry political affiliations but are elected as independents, putting the focus on individual political platforms rather than traditional party loyalties.

Caffeine fixer
Tim Hortons

Toronto's coffee culture may be blossoming but there's a long-time institution you're sure to come across: Tim Hortons. The first café was opened in Hamilton, Ontario, in 1964 by Tim Horton, then one of Canada's most famous ice-hockey stars, and the cheap-and-cheerful outfit has since grown into a chain with more than 4,400 outlets across Canada. So wherever you may be, you won't be far from a Timmy's.

Service not included
Tipping

Like US cities, Toronto is a town where tipping is essential. The minimum is usually 15 per cent of the total cost of a meal, although more generous offerings are always received with a warm thank you. A dollar or two per drink will suffice.

Last orders
Closing time

Bars and clubs are legally required to stop serving alcohol at 02.00. The majority of Torontonians seem comfortable heading home after the call for last drinks; those that want to party on head to after-hours (but dry) clubs. Finding booze after 02.00 is almost considered a sport in the city. To compensate for the early send-off, most places open early (and tend to fill up around 21.00).

If I stand here long enough someone will want a photo with me

The hardest word?
Saying sorry

Toronto is, quite rightly, regarded as one of North America's friendliest cities. Crime rates remain low and its multicultural make-up ensures that there's a warm welcome for those who arrive from elsewhere. But are Torontonians *too* nice? Given the frequency of people apologising, you'd be forgiven for thinking so. Step on someone's shoe? "Sorry." Brush against someone's shoulder? "Sorry." For many Canadians it's a simple social nicety and it

seems to work. So when you're confronted with the word – and inevitably you will be – make sure to return the favour; apologies may be given freely but they're expected in return.

Climate change
Weather

Toronto, like its urban counterparts across eastern Canada, is a place of climactic extremes, from average lows of minus 3C (excluding wind chill) in winter to highs of 21C (excluding humidity) in summer. Toronto's residents are attuned to adapting their lives according to the frivolities and cruelties of the weather. When it's bitter they head underground to utilise the Path network of stores and walkways, while warmer weather sees social lives revolving around the city's parks, outdoor swimming pools and Lake Ontario itself. Ask a passer-by what the weather will be like in a few days' time and you'll likely get an impromptu weather forecast in return.

Number crunching
Area codes

Toronto's telephone area codes begin with the number 416 – a factor that, strangely, has become a politically potent symbol in recent years. Come general election time, courting the 416 vote is an increasingly crucial part of the campaign. More recently, Toronto's superstar rapper Drake elevated the area code to a now widely used nickname for the entire city – "The 6ix" – which first appeared on his 2015 mixtape *If You're Reading This it's too Late.*

Hotels
—— At home
in Toronto

As the following pages demonstrate, Toronto's diversity extends to its mix of sleeping options, which span from luxurious storied establishments to small-scale, design-minded boutiques.

Alongside our pick of dependable global brands we've also listed the best independents that offer glimpses into the different facets of the city. Consider staying at the Drake or the Gladstone to take the pulse of the creative scene or try the Fairmont Royal York for a grand reminder of the golden era of rail travel.

Whatever you decide, expect impeccable service across the board. The stereotype is true: Canadians are very nice indeed.

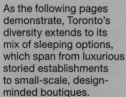

① The Windsor Arms, Yorkville
Music rooms

The Windsor Arms is a gem. Tucked away in a side alley off bustling Bloor Street, it opened in its current form in 1995 but the historic four-storey red-brick townhouse itself dates back to 1927.

The building was designed by Toronto-born architect Brian Plexton to have a central courtyard that maximises the movement of natural light; today the space hosts regular intimate performances by musicians from around the world (Andrea Bocelli performed here in 2004). The musical theme continues in the comfortable bedrooms; one of the suites even features its own baby grand piano.

High tea at The Windsor Arms is a Toronto institution and the Living Room restaurant offers a menu of slow-cooked Neapolitan-inspired fare, created by head chef Roberto Granata.
18 St Thomas Street, M5S 3E7
+1 416 971 9666
windsorarmshotel.com

MONOCLE COMMENT: Each room is stocked with a small library of classic novels and a collection of magazines and periodicals.

The Ritz-Carlton, Entertainment District
Hotel high point

The svelte 210-metre-high tower of the Ritz-Carlton dominates the heart of Toronto's entertainment district. The building was designed by New York's KPF and Toronto's Page + Steele Architects and opened in 2011.

California design agency HBA was tasked with establishing the look and feel of the 263 rooms; it opted for warm wood accents, tactile finishings and fine Frette bedlinens. The effect is a cosiness that offsets the expansive views of Lake Ontario and the city from the floor-to-ceiling windows.

On the mezzanine level you'll find Toca, the hotel's Italian restaurant; it's among Toronto's finest and overseen by Rome chef Oliver Glowig. The impressive wine cellar and selection of cheeses are particular treats.
181 Wellington Street West, M5V 3G7
+ 1 416 585 2500
ritzcarlton.com/en/hotels/canada/toronto

MONOCLE COMMENT: The on-site wellness centre is the only place in Canada where Clarin's luxurious My Blend skin analysis and tailored skin treatments are available.

③

Park Hyatt, Yorkville
Art deco elegance

The former Park Plaza Hotel (the Hyatt Group bought it in 1999) is an art deco stunner that has become synonymous with Toronto's literary history: its rooftop bar has long been a hangout for Canadian authors and it even served as the backdrop for Margaret Atwood's novel *The Edible Woman*.

Soft lighting and elegant interiors preserve the old-world charm. Smartly dressed and attentive staff are always on hand, while the rooms are furnished with pillow-top mattresses, Le Labo toiletries and snug terry bathrobes.

The 336-room high-rise features two towers: the South Tower was built in 1932 while the North Tower was added in 1955. Both provide panoramic views and are particularly resplendent when lit up at night.
4 Avenue Road, M5R 2E8
+1 416 925 1234
toronto.park.hyatt.com

MONOCLE COMMENT: Restaurant Annona is a favourite among Torontonians. Fittingly, given the venue is named after the god of harvest, chef Joan Monfaredi's menu makes the most of domestic produce and all baked goods are made in-house.

Two towers
——
The hotel is
adjoined to
a residential
building

④
Four Seasons, Yorkville
Simple yet sumptuous

The 55-storey Canadian flagship
of the Four Seasons evokes a
sense of intimacy despite its
grand scale.

Created by Toronto-based
design firm Yabu Pushelberg,
the bedrooms are simple and
sumptuous, in a refined, neutral
palette. Soundproofed walls and
windows and plush beds guarantee
a sound night's rest, while the
bathrooms feel like mini spas
thanks to the tasteful limestone-
lined walls and elegant bathtubs.
An actual spa service is available
on the ninth floor, with 17
treatment rooms, a salon and
an indoor pool.

The well-regarded Café
Boulud features menus of
reimagined French comfort
food; chef Sylvain Assié has run
the kitchens here since 2005.
60 Yorkville Avenue, M4W 0A4
+1 416 964 0411
fourseasons.com/toronto

MONOCLE COMMENT: Book an
east-facing suite overlooking the
hotel's rose-shaped garden. It was
designed by Montréal's Claude
Cormier and Associés and has
been studded with cobblestones
coloured in eight shades of red.

(5)
Hotel Le Germain Mercer,
Entertainment District
Calm oasis

Housed in a former hat factory built
in 1914, this elegant 122-room hotel
has long been popular with film-
makers during September's Toronto
International Film Festival, as well
as visitors in town for business.

Montréal-based design outfit
Lemaymichaud looked after
the lushly appointed interiors:
think felt-lined walls and original
artworks. And in waking hours
you can escape the buzz of the
streets below and enjoy the
putting green on the hotel roof
(a facility sensibly suspended
during Toronto's punishing
winter months).

The centrepiece of the hotel's
lounge bar is the stunning 4.5-
metre-high "Flower Dress" by
Canadian artist Tanya Lyons.
30 Mercer Street, M5V 1H3
+1 866 345 9501
legermainhotels.com

MONOCLE COMMENT: Victor
restaurant's complimentary
breakfasts include Montréal
bagels and Île d'Orléans jam,
while oysters are served
during its popular happy
hour (17.00 to 19.00) every
day except Sunday.

(6)
Hotel Ocho, Chinatown
Heritage accommodation

This mid-range 12-suite hotel on
Spadina Avenue is steps away from
Queen Street West, Chinatown
and Kensington Market. The pale
brick building is a heritage site – it
opened in 1902 and once served as
a textile manufacturer before being
revamped as a hotel in 2011 by its
current owner Louise Choi.

Toronto firm Dialogue 38
designed the interiors, which are
simple, clean and open plan. In the
ground-floor restaurant light floods
through floor-to-ceiling windows,
making it popular for lunch.
Executive chef Lai'ika Boulton's
menu is novel and uncomplicated,
and relies on produce sourced
from Ontario. In the evening the
cocktail bar draws workers from
nearby Bay Street.
195 Spadina Avenue, M5T 2C5
+1 416 593 0885
hotelocho.com

MONOCLE COMMENT: The orange
hotel logo is a nod to the owner's
heritage. Choi was born to Chinese
parents in South America before
moving to the Netherlands when
she was a year old. Ocho means
"eight" in Spanish, an auspicious
number in Chinese culture, and
orange is the national colour of the
Netherlands.

*Yep. The bed at
Hotel Ocho is
definitely more
comfortable
than this*

Room service
—
The hotel originally had a hospital and library

(7)

Shangri-La, Entertainment District
Glass-and-marble getaway

This glass tower soaring over University Avenue was designed by Vancouver team James Cheng and Hariri Pontarini Architects. They conceived its lobby as an "urban living room", with a Fazioli piano, a double-sided fireplace and contemporary art. Then there is the "Tea Wall", which stocks leaves from around the world, and the "Champagne Wall" with its grand range of bubbly.

The 202 bedrooms are thoughtfully designed, with accents of Italian white marble in the bathrooms and lithographic works by artist Wang Xu Yuan on the walls.

The Miraj Hammam Spa, by Caudalie Paris, offers a wide variety of treatments.
188 University Avenue, M5H 0A3
+1 647 788 8888
shangri-la.com/toronto/shangrila

MONOCLE COMMENT: The apiary on the garden terrace supplies honey to the hotel's restaurants.

⑧
The Beverley, Queen Street West
Small wonder

It can be easy to miss this tiny hotel tucked away on the lively Queen Street West shopping strip. Inside, the whitewashed walls and clean lines of the furniture keep things simple but the space still exudes an air of glamour (architect Steven Fong described the building as a work of "Rat Pack modernism", evoking Sinatra-era jet-setting elegance). There's also a popular rooftop patio.

Given the hotel's small physical footprint, it possesses a surprising sense of spaciousness. Each room also has a historic photograph of the neighbourhood on the wall, a nod to how much it has changed.
335 Queen Street West, M5V 2A1
+ 1 416 493 2786
thebeverleyhotel.ca

MONOCLE COMMENT: The restaurant is popular for brunch; we recommend the signature cocktail Beverley's Hillbilly, a concoction of bourbon, Grand Marnier and muddled raspberries.

I'm assuming birds enjoy VIP status at The Drake Hotel... or is it only ducks?

Best hotel bars

01 Thompson Hotel, Entertainment District: Boasting cabanas, an infinity pool and spectacular views, the Thompson's rooftop bar promises a memorable evening.
thompsonhotels.com

02 Fairmont Royal York, Financial District: The Royal York has not one but two of our favourite hotel bars in the city. The Library Bar features a comprehensive selection of whiskies, while the smaller Royal York Station has been designed to resemble a railway car. Both charming environments harken back to the country's colonial past.
fairmont.com/royalyork

03 The Rex, Queen Street West: This is home to what is undoubtedly one of the best jazz and blues bars in Toronto. There are live performances every night.
therex.ca

04 Park Hyatt Roof Lounge, Yorkville: This intimate space 18 floors up has an outdoor terrace where you can survey the skyline while enjoying a tasty tipple.
toronto.park.hyatt.com

Culture shock
—
The hotel is on the site of an old punk bar

Great exhibition

Capitalising on the area's lively cultural scene, the Drake hosts temporary art exhibitions and is also home to an impressive permanent collection of work by contemporary Canadian artists. It has also founded Drake AV, a collective for emerging video artists.

9
The Drake Hotel, West Queen West
Creative hub

The site of The Drake Hotel was
once a flophouse (and later, a
punk bar) before the intervention
of Toronto hotelier Jeff Stober in
2004. He envisioned a hotel that
would double as a hub for West
Queen West's artists and creatives.
  Stober had the Toronto-based
+Tongtong design studio create
a look that mixes contemporary
and vintage. The visually arresting
results include the terrazzo flooring
and brass-top bar in the lounge
and Rorschach-inspired
wood panels in the basement.
The rooms take cues from mid-
century modernism and are
well kitted out with an extensive
mini bar as well as toiletries by
New York's Malin + Goetz.
  The Drake has been drawing
visitors and residents alike to the
city's west end since it opened.
Much of this is due to its full
programme of events, ranging
from yoga workouts to trivia
nights and gigs.
1150 Queen Street West, M6J 1J3
+1 416 531 5042
thedrakehotel.ca

MONOCLE COMMENT: Pop into the
Drake General Store (*see page 48*),
which sells a huge range of "Made
in Toronto" products.

(10)

Fairmont Royal York, Financial
District
Grand design

As Canada's rail network stretched
across the continent during the
19th and 20th century, railway
companies began to build
luxurious château-style hotels
in which to accommodate the
affluent passengers traversing
the country. The Fairmont Royal
York is one such example and
remains among the city's most
evocative hotels.

Standing across from Union
Station, when it was built in 1929
it was the tallest building in the
British Commonwealth, and
despite numerous updates over the
years, notably a five-year revamp
completed in 2015, the hotel has
retained its yesteryear grandeur.

It's also worth noting that the
hotel boasts a diverse range of
eating options, including a Japanese
steakhouse, a classic English pub
and a fine-dining restaurant.
100 Front Street West, M5J 1E3
+1 416 368 2511
fairmont.com/royalyork

MONOCLE COMMENT: The prime
location means that all the major
landmarks, including the Distillery
District, harbourfront and the CN
Tower, are within walking distance.

*I think it's sad
so few people
dress up to
travel these
days*

⓫

The Hazelton, Yorkville
Former folk focus

Once the site of the Riverboat Coffee House where Joni Mitchell, Neil Young and other folk legends performed during the 1960s, the Hazelton reopened as a luxury boutique hotel in 2007.

In the foyer a striking work of stacked steel "suitcases" by Canadian artist Bruno Billio welcomes guests. For the Victorian-era building's current incarnation, Yabu Pushelberg styled the 62 rooms and 15 premium suites.

The hotel's namesake suite boasts a rotunda living room, juliet balcony and an LCD television built into the mirror in the granite-clad bathroom.
*118 Yorkville Avenue, M5R 1C2
+1 416 963 6300
thehazeltonhotel.com*

MONOCLE COMMENT: The Hazelton's Spa by Valmont features a beautiful marble-tiled indoor pool that's perfect for laps.

Gladstone Hotel

Toronto's oldest continuously run hotel is also where you can discover some of the city's most cutting-edge artwork. When Christina Zeidler took over the hotel in 2003 she dreamed up the concept of turning the 1889 Victorian establishment, designed by George Miller, into a creative hub. The hallways of guest rooms now double as galleries hosting exhibitions by both Canadian and international creatives, a number of whom are on staff at the Gladstone. "This is a social place where you can spend an afternoon, catch up with a friend and then talk to an artist," says Zeidler.

Aside from the art, the building itself is well worth a look; check out the lovingly restored frescoes and unique pillars in the Melody Bar. The rickety hand-operated lift used to ferry guests to their suites is another vintage treat.
gladstonehotel.com

On-site dining
—
Chef Mark McEwan heads the restaurant

Food and drink
—— Toronto's top tables

Restaurants
Broad palate

①
Edulis, Niagara Village
European exchange

Canada's major cities like to jostle for the title of the country's culinary capital – but Toronto has the strongest claim. With new openings nearly every week, it continues to attract some of the best chefs, sommeliers and cocktail-waiters from around the world. Toronto's multicultural population means its restaurant line-up is diverse, from novel interpretations of Canadian and US staples to some of the finest Asian, European and African cuisine in North America. If you like your food, you will like this city very much indeed.

Edulis serves French and Spanish-inspired dishes. The menu changes nearly every day, dictated by the ingredients, which are provided by nearby markets. "We're passionate about quality and we have strong relationships with our producers," says chef Michael Caballo, who opened the venture in 2012.

The five or seven-course European-influenced tasting menu is based on seafood and vegetables. On Sundays Edulis opens for lunch with a set menu and the dining room is cosy, with an outdoor space in summer.
169 Niagara Street, M5V 1C9
+1 416 703 4222
edulisrestaurant.com

Blue Monday
——
If you're banking on heading out on a Monday evening to squeeze in that last stop on your list, you may need to think again: many of the city's restaurants close on the first day of the working week.

State of the Union
The chef's own farm provides produce

② Union and Côte de Boeuf, Trinity Bellwoods
French fare

While he draws inspiration from French cooking and culture, owner and chef Teo Paul also champions freshness and a sense of the local in the two venues he owns on Ossington Avenue. At Union, a rustic-chic take on a Parisian bistro, ingredients for favourites that include the Union Salad (greens, potato rosti, chèvre and double-smoked bacon) and steak tartare are sourced from nearby farmers.

On the same street is Côte de Boeuf, a butchershop-cum-wine bar that Paul co-founded with his brother Chasen Gillies. Aside from the top-quality meat and famous rotisserie chicken, it sells a small but tidy range of groceries, charcuterie and cheese (customers can enjoy a glass of a wine and a snack while they shop or wait for their orders).

From Wednesday to Sunday the shop transforms into a *bar à vin* and the menu expands to include a few hearty meat-centric meals.
Union:
72 Ossington Avenue, M6J 2Y7
+1 416 850 0093
union72.ca
Côte de Boeuf:
130 Ossington Avenue, M6J 2Z5
+1 416 532 2333
cotedeboeuf.ca

Double duty
—
The café turns into a 'pinchos' bar at night

③
Mercat del Carmen, Trinity Bellwoods
Iberian edibles

In 2015, husband and wife Luis Valenzuela Robles Linares and Veronica Laudes opened this Spanish coffee and lunch spot to complement their more formal Iberian venue next door, Carmen. "We wanted to show a respect for food and celebrate the beauty of sharing," says Laudes. Serving lunches of sandwiches, salads and sweet treats, the café turns into a charming *pinchos* bar at night. Shelves of imported Spanish groceries, including black-truffle chips, line the shop's rear.
920 Queen Street West, M6J 1G6
+1 416 535 0404
carmensayz.com

Sausages

The city formerly known as Hogtown has a love of high-quality sausages, influenced in no small part by its longstanding German community. From high-end hot dogs to some mouthwatering wurst, get your fix at these places.

01 Otto's Berlin Döner, Kensington Market:
This street-food sit-down located in busy Kensington Market is perfect for a quick currywurst and pils, or a wiener and *weisse*.
ottosdoner.com

02 Fancy Franks, citywide:
The humble hot dog is elevated with gourmet flourishes at this popular chain (there are three shops dotted across the city). Squeaky curds also feature heavily on the menu.
fancyfranks.com

03 Wvrst, King Street West:
This beer-and-cider hall's long tables create an upbeat atmosphere to sample some of the city's best wurst.
wvrst.com

④

The Commodore, Parkdale
Comfort-food cruise

The Commodore is a restaurant and cocktail bar with a seafood focus. The charming space was designed in 2015 to resemble a ship's hull: faux vaulted ceilings were added to the exposed brick walls and the lights dotted in the ceiling above the bar were salvaged from a 1957 cruise ship. "We wanted to maintain that lived-in feel, polished but still rough around the edges," says manager and co-owner Jason Romanoff.

The ingredients are gathered from Ontario and dishes cover everything from reimagined comfort food to French and Asian flavours. The brunch menu is also a hit; fluffy pancakes are served with espresso syrup and topped with creamy tiramisu mousse. The Reuben eggs benedict is a triumph too. The drip coffee is made with Sam James coffee beans *(see page 34).*
1265 Queen Street West, M6K 1L4
+1 416 537 1265
commodorebar.ca

For impressing clients

01 **Branca, Little Portugal:** Argentinian eats and cocktails await in an old brick residence. Not surprisingly, meat is the drawcard: it's cooked in a barbecue hut out the back over an *asado*-style fire pit.
branca.ca

02 **Dandylion, Queen Street West:** Large industrial windows create a light, airy feel at this vegetable-focused restaurant.
restaurantdandylion.com

⑤

Julie's Cuban Restaurant, Trinity Bellwoods
Revamped and romantic

This dining room on leafy Dovercourt Road is one of Toronto's romantic venues. Opened in 1954, it served workers from the nearby (now-defunct) bread factory until 1997. Sylvia Llewellyn, daughter of founder Julie, took over and transformed it, retaining the original faded signage ("Julie's Snack Bar"). Sylvia's Cuban husband, Jesus Baute, heads the kitchen and produces an unfussy menu of blue-marlin ceviche, creamy housemade guacamole and classic *ropa vieja* pulled-steak stew.
202 Dovercourt Road, M6J 3C8
+1 416 532 7397
juliescuban.com

Must-try
California chicken bao from Almighty Bao, Trinity Bellwoods
Chef Taylor Gilbert takes great pride in dishes that defy tradition and this is a prime example. The steamed-milk buns, delivered fresh daily, are larger than normal, making them a meal in themselves. Instead of pork there's a panko-crusted chicken breast topped with bacon, fried shallots, a slice of seaweed and pickled cucumber. Combined they create a unique flavour that will have you returning for more.
1212 Dundas Street West

6
Farmhouse Tavern,
Junction Triangle
Season's eatings

The Farmhouse Tavern serves
brunch staples and homely dinners.
Owner Darcy MacDonell started
the restaurant in 2012 and the
menu, which uses ingredients from
the province's food producers,
changes with the season.

The drinks list features
Canadian craft beers and Ontario
vintages from the wineries of
Niagara, Point Pelee and Prince
Edward County. The space, with
its reclaimed sliding barn doors,
is as evocative of life beyond the
city as its name suggests.
1627 Dupont Street, M6P 3S8
+ 1 416 561 9114
farmhousehospitality.tumblr.com

Quick eats

01 The Pie Commission, Trinity Bellwoods: This small shopfront on Dundas West has earned its crust as one of the easiest and tastiest options for an impromptu picnic in nearby Trinity Bellwoods Park.
piecommission.com

02 Bobbie Sue's Mac + Cheese, Trinity Bellwoods: This mac shack is located just off Ossington on Foxley, and serves hot tins of macaroni and cheese from a colourful counter right out on the pavement.
bobbiesues.com

03 California Sandwiches, citywide: The breaded-veal sandwich has a cult-like following due to its heaped portion of Ontario-raised veal and homemade tomato sauce.
eatcalifornia.ca

04 Porchetta & Co, Trinity Bellwoods and Entertainment District: Certainly not gluten (nor glutton) free, Porchetta & Co's pork sandwiches can be found on both Dundas Street West and King Street West. Order the classic house special.
porchettaco.com

05 Seven Lives Tacos, Kensington Market: This cash-only Baja-style taquería offers limited seating to enjoy its prized fish tacos inside; they are better enjoyed one block over on the grassy lawn in Bellevue Square.
69 Kensington Avenue

06 Harbord Fish and Chips, Harbord Village: You can try your luck at reeling in cosy seating at this chippy, tucked away on cheerful Harbord, or get your catch to go (in newspaper wrapping).
+1 416 925 2225

⑦ The Black Hoof, Trinity Bellwoods
Meating spot

The Black Hoof is cosy with a refined edge: its owner, Jen Agg, describes the restaurant's offerings as "deliciously meat and off-cut-centric but always with lighter options available". Ingredients are provided by a range of organic and biodynamic companies and farmers, which means the menu changes frequently. Inside, the slim restaurant has sleek marble countertops, a rustic wooden chalkboard menu and glamorous mirrors. As Agg says, it is "lit with an eye to making people look like their best selves".
928 Dundas Street West, M6J 1W3
+1 416 551 8854
theblackhoof.com

I'm a dog eating a hot dog. It's very meta

⑧ Oddseoul, Trinity Bellwoods
Late-night fusion

Brothers Leeto and Leemo Han, who were raised in Philadelphia, opened Oddseoul in 2013. Melding South Korean staples with favourites from their hometown, Oddseoul's small sharing plates are imaginative delights. The lipsmacking Bulgogi cheese-steak sandwich, the delicious Buffalo tofu and the seared mackerel (blackened with a blowtorch at the table) are standouts.

The space resembles an old warehouse; most of the fixtures and furniture were sourced from a friend's junkyard. If you don't mind the loud music, Oddseoul is also one of the city's best late-night dining options (the kitchen closes at 02.00).
90 Ossington Avenue, M6J 2Z4

The bats seem to be out for a late dinner too…

⑨ Cluny Bistro, Distillery District
Modern classics

Soft music, classic bistro chairs and dinner plates adorned with toile-inspired designs make Cluny one of Toronto's finest French-dining options. Classic dishes have been modernised and draw inspiration from former French colonies Vietnam and Algeria.

"Our house bread, fresh seafood and wine lists have become inherent in the culture of our restaurant," says general manager Jean-Valery Lacasse. The list of wines is strong too; attentive wait staff will direct you to the best choice to accompany your meal.
35 Tank House Lane, M5A 3C4
+1 416 203 2632
clunybistro.com

Must-try
Nduja sausage pizza
from Pizzeria Libretto,
Trinity Bellwoods
This venue was established in 2008 before the Ossington strip was a haven for the hip. The sausage pizza is particularly tasty; the meat is whey-fed pork from Burkefield Farms, seasoned to perfection and baked for less than 90 seconds in the wood-fired oven to guarantee the classic charred crust. Try pairing it with a glass of gragnano, the chilled, sparkling red wine traditionally served in pizzerias in Naples.
pizzerialibretto.com

⑩

The Walton, Little Italy
Cosy cocktails

The Walton is a charming café by day and a romantic cocktail bar by night. "We'll let you drink in the day too," says Alison MacKenna, who set up the bar with her husband Sunny Yoanidis in 2015. The intimate space has the quiet glamour of a French bistro, the ease of a British pub and the joie de vivre, at night at least, of an old jazz club. Chairs sourced from an old fish-and-chip shop add to the informal atmosphere.

French pastries from The Tempered Room are served each morning and a worthy selection of bar snacks, including charcuterie and pickled fish, is available at night. The Elderflower Royale is a refreshing choice from The Walton's simple cocktail menu; if it's a sunny evening sip it outside in the leafy courtyard at the back of the bar.
607 College Street, M6G 1B5
+1 647 352 5520
thewalton607.com

⑪

Actinolite, Christie Pits
Neighbourhood favourite

Actinolite is operated by husband-and-wife team Justin Cournoyer and Claudia Bianchi. It opened in 2012 and the small but perfectly formed space feels like eating at a friend's home, a vibe that's intensified by the fact that Bianchi and Cournoyer live upstairs.

Diners can pick between two multicourse menus or the two-courses-and-glass-of-wine "neighbourhood" option. "The food we serve changes according to what's in season, fresh and available," says Bianchi, "not just for the sake of change".
971 Ossington Avenue, M6G 3V5
+1 416 962 8943
actinoliterestaurant.com

⑫

Piano Piano, The Annex
Famiglia fun

The name of this restaurant comes from an Italian phrase suggesting slow and steady wins the race. It reflects the desire of co-owners and couple Victor Barry and Nikki Leigh McKean to create a place where diners can take their time and savour the company of friends and family.

This focus also comes through the menu of hearty traditional classics (think bone-in veal parmesan and spicy Sicilian pizza) and the kid-pleasing Piccolo Piano room stocked with games, books, and a vintage *Pac-Man* arcade game.
88 Harbord Street, M5S 1G5
+1 416 929 7788
pianopianotherestaurant.com

Coffee shops

The finest examples of the outlets that keep this bustling city bright-eyed and bushy-tailed.

01 Sam James Coffee Bar, Little Italy: The name Sam James has become synonymous with quality coffee across Toronto, though its first location on Harbord still stands out for its particularly cosy interior and well-crafted cups.
samjamescoffeebar.com

02 White Squirrel Coffee Shop, Trinity Bellwoods: This café sits at the southern edge of Trinity Bellwoods Park and takes its name from the white squirrels that live there.
whitesquirrelcoffee.com

03 Quantum Coffee, Entertainment District: Winter visitors to this coffee shop can order its famous crème brûlée cappuccino, a frothy concoction with a carefully caramelised top.
quantumcoffee.io

04 Boxcar Social, Summerhill: Coffee and craft brews are standouts at this east-end café-bar, so you can decide on something tasty to pick you up or wind you down.
boxcarsocial.ca

05 Cherry Bomb, Roncesvalles Village: This unpretentious and bright café is a staple for residents of the Roncesvalles area, many of whom bring their own mug for a friendly discount.
cherrybombcoffee.ca

06 Crafted, Trinity Bellwoods: Crafted has mastered the art of coffee-brewing every which way, attracting those in search of a pour-over, French-press or famed six-hour cold-drip coffee.
pilotcoffeeroasters.com

⑬
Kinka Izakaya, Church and Wellesley
Share nicely

Kinka Izakaya's first location introduced Japanese small-plate dining to Toronto in 2009. Since then its elegant communal dining rooms have opened at two further locations in Toronto, with additional outposts in Montréal and Tokyo. The innovative menu of sharing plates – including the delightful salmon *tataki* and indulgent deep-fried brie – fuses modern and traditional cooking methods. The drinks offering is a treat as well; the selection of premium saké is among the best in the city.
398 Church Street, M5B 2A2
+ 1 416 977 0999
kinkaizakaya.com

⑭

Peter Pan Bistro, Queen Street West
Toronto institution

Peter Pan opened in 1936, so the city that's come to love it held its breath when the bistro closed for renovation and reopened under the stewardship of executive chef Noah Goldberg in 2015. Goldberg's seasonal menus are inspired by French and British fare and don't stray too far from the classic dishes that have made the restaurant a staple in the city for decades.

The interior is charming: many of the original art deco fixtures have been restored, including a handsome bar, romantic dining booths and a striking ceiling, which are fitting tributes to the venue's storied past. Unusual tapestries by UK artist Debbie Lawson add an element of whimsy to the interior. The beautiful second-floor dining room – featuring beautiful original stained-glass windows – is available for private hire.
373 Queen Street West, M5V 2A4
+1 416 792 3838
peterpanbistro.ca

⑮

Sud Forno, Trinity Bellwoods
Idyllic Italian

Sud Forno features a traditional Italian-style bakery on its groundfloor, offering superb takeaway options and fine imported produce; on its upper floor is a long table for communal dining. We recommend the Pizza Cosí with porcini mushrooms and prosciutto di parma.

It's one of several Toronto restaurants overseen by Cosimo Mammoliti and Paolo Scoppio. They began selling Italian staples in a shop called Terroni a few blocks away; it's now their flagship site.
716 Queen Street West, M6J 1E8
+1 416 504 7667
sudforno.com

⑯

Yasu, Harbord Village
Raw talent

Chef and owner Yasuhisa Ouchi had years of experience making sushi – he began in Osaka at 16 and then worked in Melbourne – before creating his own dine-in restaurant in Harbord Village. Ouchi knew he wanted his own restaurant where he could connect with his patrons and create fresh dishes in front of their eyes.

The interior echoes the food that is served: compact yet generous, simple yet elegant. There is no unnecessary pomp and every detail, from the number of barstools to the sparse and considered garnish, feels perfectly thought out. Favourite nigiri include the monkfish liver and sea urchin, though all food is served

omakase-style, meaning the chef will determine your meal based on his freshest favourites that evening.

Despite the immense care and expertise that Ouchi puts into his dishes, he still values socialising with diners as much as creating delicious fare. "We look very serious when preparing sushi but we are always happy to chat and answer questions."
81 Harbord Street, M5S 1G4
+1 416 477 2361
yasu-sushibar.com

⑰

Buca, Entertainment District
Meaty morsels

With one half underground in a former boiler-room, Buca is one of the most beguiling fine-dining establishments in Toronto. Chefs Rob Gentile and Andrew Halitski are proponents of the "nose to tail" school of cookery with excellent results; try the crispy pigs' ears, the duck-offal ragu or the *cervello* (bacon and sage-wrapped fried lambs' brains). Each is a triumph.

We recommend asking to be seated at the long communal tables in the smaller dining room at the back of the restaurant: you'll have a fine view of the glass-fronted wine cellar.

Buca now boasts two more venues: a full-menu restaurant in Yorkville and a small snack bar (called Bar Buca) one block south along Portland Street.
604 King Street West, M5V 1M6
+1 416 865 1600
buca.ca

(18)
The Federal, Little Portugal
Quiet achiever

This low-key venue is open for brunch and dinner but no matter the time, diners clamour for its famous burger: Four Guys. It's all in the technique: a ball of freshly ground beef is flattened with a steak press, sealing in the juices and creating a rich brown crust.
1438 Dundas Street West, M6J 1Y6
+1 647 352 9120
thefed.ca

(19)
Miku Toronto, Financial District
Sushi with a twist

Aburi Restaurants opened this 200-cover venue specialising in *aburi* (part grilled, part raw) sushi in 2015. Located in the RBC building, the sleek glass-walled space is favoured by those entertaining business clients.

The Aburi Oshi sushi plates starring flame-seared British Columbian salmon, *saba* (mackerel) and *ebi* (prawn) are popular. A raw bar serves delicacies such as oysters from Prince Edward Island.

Miku also bottles its own water and donates the proceeds from sales to a local charity.
105-10 Bay Street, M5J 2R8
+1 647 347 7347
mikutoronto.com

Business lunches

01 Jump, Financial District: This business staple is overseen by Vancouver-born chef Luke Kennedy. He's renowned for his charcoal-cooked meats and handmade pastas.
jumprestaurant.com

02 Canoe, Financial District: Don't be put off by the somewhat fussy presentation of the plates: executive chef John Horne, an alumnus of London's Almeida, creates ambitious food inspired by Canadian produce. It's a good option if you're seeking to impress.
canoerestaurant.com

03 The Chase, Financial District: This sleek restaurant boasts impressive views across the city and is widely regarded as one of the finest seafood restaurants in Toronto. It's headed by executive chef Michael Steh, who developed his passion for quality Canadian produce while growing up in rural Oshawa, Ontario.
thechasetoronto.com

⑳
Scaramouche, Casa Loma
Discreet charm

Scaramouche has been a standard-bearer for fine dining since it opened its doors in 1980. And for the vast majority of that time, British-born, publicity-shy chef and owner Keith Froggett has been in the kitchen overseeing the offering of fine, unfussy fare.

The simple and smart dining room attracts business travellers, former prime ministers and those with something to celebrate. A must-try dish is the famed coconut cream pie: Froggett has attempted to take it off the menu at times but the public outcry always forces its return. Another drawcard is the enviable view of the Toronto skyline from the dining room.

Scaramouche's less-formal sister venue, The Pasta Bar & Grill, operates in an adjacent space. Reservations for both are essential.
1 Benvenuto Place, M4V 2L1
+1 416 961 8011
scaramoucherestaurant.com

It's all gravy

The French-Canadian poutine contains the same three elements, whether dressed-up or down: crisp french fries, warm gravy and chewy cheese curds. Cheese curds, by the way, are a speciality in Canada – they are the byproduct of pasteurised milk.
poutini.com

Brunch spots
Get in early

①

Aunties & Uncles, Harbord Village
Simple but effective

If you feel like you're at a close
relative's house while eating at
this beloved brunch spot, you
won't be the only one. Owner Russ
Nicholls started the restaurant out
of his apartment (upstairs from
the current location), where he
would serve nine diners at a time.
The space has obviously expanded
since but still retains its cosy and
convivial atmosphere.

The no-fuss food is served in
large portions. "Most restaurant
chefs and owners think they're
too good to serve a basic meal
to people; the food all has to be
tied into a knot or something,"
says Nicholls.

Bits of Canadiana can be
spotted on the walls, including
tear-outs of old hockey players
that Nicholls found in a scrapbook,
and a sign for Sunny Bar, a diner
that used to exist in The Junction
neighbourhood. It's easy to see
why that particular sign is one
of Nicholls's favourites; he views
the old diner in the same way he
hopes the city sees his own: "It's
authentic and it's old and it's just
part of Toronto."
74 Lippincott Street, M5S 2P1
+1 416 324 1375
auntiesanduncles.ca

The Caesar

If Canada had a national
cocktail, the Caesar would be it.
Essentially a bloody mary, the
glass rim is spiced with chilli
and other seasonings but
there's one crucial twist:
Clamato juice made with real
clam broth. The following are
purveyors of the city's finest.

01 The Federal, Little
Portugal: A favourite in
Monocle's Toronto bureau,
the Caesar at The Federal
(see page 36) is made from
Walter Caesar Mix and
has Cool Ranch Doritos
crushed around the rim.
thefed.ca

02 The County General,
Trinity Bellwoods: Dill-
infused Clamato is the
twist in the offering from
The County General *(see
page 40)*, which is best
enjoyed on their slim patio.
thecountygeneral.ca

03 Dundas & Carlaw,
Leslieville: The Caesar here
will sate hunger and thirst
with a pepperette and
pickled-vegetable skewer.
dundasandcarlaw.com

Brunch hotspot
—
To bag a table, be sure to arrive early

② Saving Grace, Trinity Bellwoods
Bewitching breakfasts

When Monica Miller opened Saving Grace in 2000 it was the lone café-cum-brunch spot on this part of the Dundas West strip. "I wanted to be in a neighbourhood that needed me," she says. "I'm obsessed with the magic of food."

It's since become one of the city's most popular breakfast venues. As well as a specials menu there's a regular menu that always incorporates thoughtful twists on brunch favourites. Most ingredients come from nearby Kensington Market and the streetside markets of Chinatown, where Miller shops every morning.
907 Dundas Street West, M6J 1V9
+1 416 703 7368

③ Mitzi's, Roncesvalles Village
Always glad you came

This friendly neighbourhood haunt has been around since 1995, surrounded by old homes and tall trees. "We're a bit like Cheers," says co-owner Michael Watson. "We know our customers by name and they know us." He and his partner Jason Bradfield were regular diners at Mitzi's before buying it in 2012.

The menu changes every week. While there are always brunch staples, they are never prepared the same way; the oatmeal pancakes are a particular treat. Everything is homemade and the ingredients are sourced nearby.
100 Sorauren Avenue, M6R 2C9
+1 416 588 1234
mitziscafe.com

④ Rose and Sons Swan, Trinity Bellwoods
Dive on in

Closing in 2015 after more than 17 years of service, the iconic Swan diner and bar was given a new lease on life by Anthony Rose, one of Toronto's most celebrated restaurateurs. Rose, who owns and operates a number of restaurants around the city, including his eponymous Rose and Sons diner in Midtown, had a soft spot for the Swan and saw its potential.

There's boisterous chatter at the counter and intimate discussions in booths. And the updated menu stays true to its diner roots.
892 Queen Street West, M6J 1G3
+1 647 342 0356
roseandsons.ca

⑤
The County General,
Trinity Bellwoods
Southern hospitality

Drawing inspiration from the southern US, this restaurant serves a small, well-curated menu of hearty fare, crafted by owner Carlo Catallo. From house-spiced fried chicken to little baskets of crispy pig ears to snack on, the creations allow the ingredients to sing.

The burgers, made with Canadian dry-aged beef, are something special – wash them down with a Caesar *(see page 38)*. There is a second location in the Riverside neighbourhood.
936 Queen Street West, M6J 1G9
+1 416 531 4447
thecountygeneral.ca

Bakeries

01 **Prairie Boy Bread, Little Portugal:** Organic sourdough loaves – made from recipes from the Canadian Prairies – aren't the only attraction at this bakery's permanent space on College: it also serves coffee, homemade cinnamon rolls, jam and chutney, and Toronto-made kitchen accessories.
prairieboyfarms. wordpress.com

02 **Harbord Bakery, Harbord Village:** Perhaps downtown Toronto's best-known Jewish bakery, this is the perfect spot for a loaf of challah or the rolled chocolate rugelach.
harbordbakery.ca

03 **Forno Cultura, King West Village:** Don't be fooled by this bakery's modern appearance: Forno Cultura serves Italian baked goods using family recipes dating back three generations.
fornocultura.com

Diners
Casual bites

①
Pancer's Original Deli,
Wilson Heights
Candy store

Opened in 1957 by Moe Pancer and his son Stan, this Jewish deli remains a Toronto institution. Its recently renovated, canteen-like dining room is as popular with the city's great and good (the Toronto Maple Leafs are regularly spotted here, as was the late Canadian comedian John Candy) as it is with those who've dined here for years.

The menu is crammed with classics: the cured-meat sandwiches are a favourite, as are the heaped plates of cabbage rolls, steaming bowls of matzo-ball soup and the fabled cheese *blintz* (a crêpe stuffed with sweetened ricotta and dressed with sour cream and blueberry jam). Come early: the queues to get a table tend to be lengthy.
3856 Bathurst Street, M3H 3N4
+1 416 636 1230
pancersoriginaldeli.com

②
The Lakeview Restaurant,
Trinity Bellwoods
Day or night

Since opening in 1932 The Lakeview has served diner fare, from North American breakfast classics to its wildly popular cornflake-chicken sandwich. It became one of the city's few 24-hour diners in 2008, retaining much of the original interior, including the bar stools and booths.

"We're a part of Toronto's past, present and future," says manager Susan DeFreitas. "It's a safe space where everyone is welcome." Tom Cruise fans may want to pay homage: the 1988 classic *Cocktail* was filmed here.
1132 Dundas Street West, M6J 1X2
+1 416 850 8886
thelakeviewrestaurant.ca

③
The Senator, Yonge-Dundas
Maintaining the buzz

The Senator is the oldest restaurant in Toronto. Opened in 1929 as the Busy Bee just off Yonge Street, it has retained much of its historic charm. Mahogany booths flank the wall opposite the long counter, with lighting fixtures from the 1940s. "There's not a lot of change on the menu," admits general manager Anne Hollyer. "There's a comfort level to continuity; I think that's why people keep coming back."

The Senator makes full use of ingredients from the surrounding area: milk from Caledon, Ontario, salmon that's smoked in-house, and maple syrup produced in Kingston. The fabled Senator breakfast is the star draw here: bacon and egg with challah toast, maple cider baked beans and home fries, and tea or coffee with organic milk. You'll be hard-pressed to find a heartier meal to start your day.
249 Victoria Street, M5B 1V8
+1 416 364 7517
thesenator.com

(4)
Caplansky's, Harbord Village
Delightful delicatessen

Zane Caplansky began selling his
smoked-meat sandwiches out of
The Monarch Tavern in 2008.
Lacking kitchen space, he smoked
the briskets in his backyard. It didn't
take long for the deli delights to hit
the road, becoming Toronto's first
modern food-truck phenomenon.

In 2009 Caplansky sparked a
delicatessen revival in Downtown
when he opened this venue. "My
family's been in the business for
four generations," he says. "My
great-grandmother used to make
corned beef and pickled-tongue
sandwiches for garment workers."
356 College Street, M5T 1S6
+1 416 500 3852
caplanskys.com

*I asked for
a triple serve
of brisket...*

5

Hastings Snack Bar, Leslieville
Polished Polish

When the owner of Hastings Snack Bar retired after 53 years, Karolina Conroy, who owns the barbershop next door, took it over. She updated the space with wood and exposed-brick accents and restored the original bar stools and countertop.

Enlisting the help of her mother, she serves a small menu of traditional Polish breakfasts and lunches, including *pierogi* (dumplings), cabbage rolls, *paczki* (doughnuts) and home-baked pastries. With a chalkboard menu and a charming stained-glass window façade, this is one of the most inviting of the city's no-frills options.
5 Hastings Avenue, M4L 2L1
+1 416 896 1466

Pole position
——
Start your day with a Polish breakfast

Drinks
Bar trek

①

Bellwoods Brewery, Trinity
Bellwoods
Ringing endorsement

Bellwoods Brewery is perhaps the
city's most beloved craft brewer.
Each of its beers has a unique
character and personality – and
many also boast cult followings.
We recommend the Witchshark,
an imperial IPA with a name that
references its bite: it's both bitter
and high in alcohol content (9 per
cent). There's a well-crafted menu
too, and you can grab a drink or
two to go from the bottle shop. The
distinctive beer labels are designed
by Doublenaut and printed by Kid
Icarus (*see page 61*).
124 Ossington Avenue, M6J 2Z5
+1 416 535 4586
bellwoodsbrewery.com

②
Bar Raval, Little Italy
Reassuringly 'familia'

Opened in 2015, this elevated
Spanish tapas and cocktail bar has
become one of Toronto's most
talked-about watering holes. It is
Bar Raval's interior, as much as
the Basque-inspired menu of small
tasting dishes, that has had people
flocking across the threshold.
The warm, undulating mahogany
room, created by Toronto-based
firm Partisans, was inspired by the
oeuvre of Antoni Gaudí.
  We recommend any of the
octopus dishes washed down with
a glass of Give Me Back the Nights:
a bourbon-based cocktail mixed
with squid ink.
505 College Street, M6G 1A4
thisisbarraval.com

③
The Oxley, Yorkville
Brit hit

Opened in 2012 in the elegant
Yorkville neighbourhood, The Oxley
is a thoughtful re-interpretation
of a British gastro pub. It's a
popular choice among business
travellers seeking a more homely
place to talk shop than the glitzier
venues Downtown.
  Chef Andrew Carter has created
a menu of comfort food, from roast
duck with mushroom *pithivier* (a
type of pie) to UK classics such as
fish and chips and rarebit. Parent
company Broadcloth Hospitality
also owns The Queen & Beaver
and The Wickson Social pubs.
121 Yorkville Avenue, M5R 1C4
+1 647 348 1300
theoxley.com

Hmmm, I can't
quite taste
the terroir...
better order
another bottle

(4)

Midfield Wine Bar & Tavern,
Little Portugal
Best cellar

This pared-back bar is a
little deceptive: based on first
impressions you wouldn't assume
it's home to one of the city's
most extensive wine lists. But its
cellars are fully stocked with a bias
towards vintages from heritage
vineyards and smaller boutique
wineries around the world.

The simple French-inspired
food has been created to
complement the wines, says
manager Irene Dongas (*pictured*).
But it's the wine cellar that's the
main attraction.
*1434 Dundas Street West, M6J 1Y7
+1 647 345 7005*

⑤
Bar Begonia, The Annex
Casual but elegant

The fifth establishment from restaurateur duo Anthony Rose and Robert Wilder, Bar Begonia is furnished with marble tabletops and a curvaceous wooden bar. Its menu of rustic French classics is inspired by Rose's time spent in Paris.

"The menu changes almost monthly but there are a few favourites that always stay," says chef Trista Sheen. Among them is the enormously popular lemon tart. The drinks list is refreshed regularly too; general manager Oliver Stern and bar manager Veronica Saye are always innovating.
252 Dupont Street, M5R 1V3
+1 647 352 3337
barbegonia.com

⑥
DaiLo, Little Italy
Delicacies meet design

DaiLo's head chef Nick Liu has pored over the details of his French-inspired Chinese restaurant since it opened its doors in 2014. The dishes, such as the delicious whole trout, are considered and playful. The interior is communal but maintains a sense of intimacy too: the ornate screening that divides the restaurant's booths means you can share a private evening without feeling secluded from the rest of the room. Upstairs is its sister dim sum and cocktail bar LoPan. A slightly more casual affair than its older sibling, it serves until 02.00.
503 College Street, M6J 2J3
+1 647 341 8882
dailoto.com

Independent breweries
—
01 Left Field Brewery
Baseball-themed joint.
leftfieldbrewery.ca
02 Duggan's Brewery
Small-batch speciality beer.
duggansbreweryparkdale.com
03 Indie Ale House
Flavourful, full-bodied beer.
indiealehouse.com

⑦
Archive, Trinity Bellwoods
Grape expectations

Brothers Josh and Joel Corea opened Archive to broaden Toronto's wine palate. "If you're interested in learning more about wine you can do it here," says Josh, a former teacher whose past career is echoed by the space's old-school chairs. By exploring lesser-known winemaking regions, sommelier Josh (*pictured above*) has sourced a diverse selection that you won't find anywhere else in the city. A Mediterranean-style snack menu, made with ingredients from Ontario and Québec, includes meat cured in-house.
909 Dundas Street West, M6J 1V9
+1 647 748 0909
archive909.com

⑧
Communist's Daughter, Trinity Bellwoods
Dive-bar delight

Don't be put off by the Communist's Daughter's rather ramshackle appearance: this is one of Toronto's most charming dive bars. From the mix-and-match linoleum tabletops to the well-worn jukebox and the frayed lace curtains in the window, you'd be forgiven for thinking it hasn't changed much since its former incarnation as a Portuguese diner (the latter's original "Nazaré Snack Bar" sign still looms, in all its faded glory, above the front door).

The crowd is mixed: Toronto's bright young things mingle at the candlelit tables with those who've been drinking here for years. Live bands play in the storefront window on Saturday and Sunday nights, and on Mondays patrons are encouraged to bring in their favourite vinyl, the merits of which are put to a lively public vote at the end of the A-side.
1149 Dundas Street West, M6J 1X4
+1 647 435 0103

⑨

Rhum Corner, Trinity Bellwoods
Taste of the Caribbean

Owner Jen Agg describes Rhum
Corner as a "mini Caribbean
vacation" and styled the bright
interiors on her husband Roland
Jean's recollections of his childhood
in Haiti. As its name suggests, the
bar has one of the most extensive
selections of rum in Toronto – 100
varieties to be exact. Artworks by
Jean adorn the walls.

A pounding soundtrack of
Haitian *kompa* and *rara* music
and the playful drinks list (which
includes frescoes and slushies),
add to the lively atmosphere.
926 Dundas Street West, M6J 1W3
+ 1 647 346 9356
rhumcorner.com

⑩

Black Dice Café, Little Portugal
Japanese rockabilly

When his collection of 1950s
and 1960s US memorabilia began
to overwhelm his small Toronto
home, Hideki Saito (*pictured*)
decided to mix work and play. And
so, in 2009, he opened Black Dice
Café as a Japanese rockabilly bar.

Americana may dominate the
decor – the walls are decked with
old vinyl and vintage film posters,
complemented by the popular

jukebox and pinball machine – but
the drinks here are exclusively
Japanese. A good range of beers
– both bottled and on tap – rubs
shoulders with a fine selection of
whiskies and saké.

While the kitschy bar has its
fans on the basis of its eccentric
decor alone, ask most regular
patrons why they keep returning
and the response is invariably an
enthusiastic "*Hideki!*"
1574 Dundas Street West, M6K 1T8
+ 1 647 748 1574
blackdicecafe.com

⑪

Lula Lounge, Little Portugal
Sultry salsa

Lula Lounge grew from informal
dance lessons and community
arts events hosted by friends Jose
Ortega and Jose Nieves in their
Toronto apartment. Today it is one
of the liveliest jazz and salsa spots
in the city. Acts from around the
world regularly perform here, and
a busy schedule of spirited salsa
classes means that the dancefloor is
rarely empty. Illuminated by sultry
black and red lighting, it plays host
to boisterous salsa bands every
Friday and Saturday. Its colourful
sign, high over the front door, is a
neighbourhood landmark.
1585 Dundas Street West, M6J 1T9
+ 1 416 588 0307
lula.ca

Retail
—— Top shops

From fashion and homeware to vinyl and books, Torontonians are zealous champions of small business. Wherever you are in the city, chances are an independent retailer is lurking right around the corner. This penchant for keeping things on an intimate scale has resulted in a blossoming eco-system for homegrown and global makers and artisans, who enjoy the freedom to trial new products and designs.

We've scoured every neighbourhood to find the establishments showcasing the best in terms of concept, product offering and service. Over the next few pages you'll find a thoughtful general store, a 19th-century inspired apothecary and even a bookshop outfitted with a vending machine that dispenses rare books.

So be sure to save some luggage space – you're bound to want to take a piece of Toronto home with you.

Concept stores
Ideas people

①
Drake General Store,
West Queen West
Talking points

As the retail arm of The Drake Hotel (*see page 23*), Drake General Store stays true to its brand by stocking everything from glassware and dark-rum-scented candles to Toronto-themed children's T-shirts. But there is a method to the madness. "We choose items for their ability to spark conversation," says co-founder Joyce Lo.

The store features hard-to-find brands such as Puebco but also creates its own products under several labels, including Arborist. Its new digs across from the hotel include a permanent space for the popular Kensington Market barbershop Crows Nest and an area for art exhibitions and pop-up shops. If you're peckish, an in-store café serves coffee, tea and snacks.
1151 Queen Street West, M6J 0A8
+1 647 346 0742
drakegeneralstore.ca

②

The Lucky Penny General Store
& Café, Trinity Bellwoods
Essentials and more

The Lucky Penny General Store
& Café was inspired by a shop
that sold "a little bit of everything"
that owner Debbie Rix used to
visit as a child. In her attempt to
revive the Toronto tradition of
the neighbourhood cornershop,
Rix stocks her space with a highly
varied selection of items. Along
with essential groceries such as
mustard and eggs you'll also find
children's toys and tennis balls
for the courts at nearby Trinity
Bellwoods Park.

Rix also tries to ensure she
carries Toronto products, such as
bread from Kensington Market's
Blackbird Bakery and locally made
dog treats. A bonus is the lovely
streetside patio – it's a great spot to
enjoy an ice cream or Americano
and watch the bikes whizz by on
the nearby Shaw Street bike path.
189 Shaw Street, M6J 2W7
+ 1 416 516 9666

3

Old Faithful, Trinity Bellwoods
Minimalist chic

Old Faithful is co-founder Walter Manning's antidote to the culture of fast consumerism. "We source everyday items that are crafted from natural materials, built to last through the generations," he says. After setting up shop in Vancouver, Manning opened this Toronto outpost near Trinity Bellwoods Park in 2015. Customers are warmly welcomed into the freshly scented and whitewashed space, where homeware products ranging from ceramic bowls to woollen throws are immaculately arranged on the wooden tables and shelves.
886 Queen Street West, M6J 1G3
+1 647 352 9376
oldfaithfulshop.com

Retail neighbourhoods

01 Junction: This formerly blue-collar neighbourhood, northwest of Downtown, is having a retail resurgence thanks to the droves of designers and young professionals who now call the area home. It's known for its solid mix of design and furniture shops.

02 Dundas West: It's a pity Dundas West is often overshadowed by busier Queen Street to the south. From Bookhou – where totes and homeware products are made on-site – to womenswear retailer Comrags, this relaxed street has some of the city's most interesting independent businesses and emerging designers.

03 Parkdale: The western end of Queen Street West, starting from Dufferin, is known as Parkdale. It was once an unsavoury part of town but gentrification has brought excellent restaurants as well as retail offerings from fashion to homeware.

04 Ossington: The north-south strip of Ossington Avenue makes up for its relatively small real-estate footprint with an array of retail options. Whether it's Jonathan + Olivia's (*see page 52*) selection of clothing from European and US designers or fine tableware from VdeV, there's bound to be something that will make you want to open your wallet.

05 Yorkville: North of Bloor Street, Yorkville caters to the affluent neighbourhoods that surround it. The streets here are studded with boutiques including 119 Corbo, Capsule and Pomp & Pageantry.

④
Monocle Shop, Little Italy
Drop in to our place

Our Canadian home follows the same shop-bureau format as our outposts in Hong Kong, Tokyo and Singapore. Observe our team members as they busy themselves with stories for forthcoming issues (feel free to drop in with any tip-offs) and browse the full range of products and collaborations with our favourite partners, such as Porter, Delfonics and Comme des Garçons. It's also where you can plug the gaps in your collection of past issues of MONOCLE and choose from our expanding collection of books.
776 College Street, M6G 1C6
+ 1 647 694 2626
monocle.com

⑤
Souvenir, Little Portugal
Stripped-back showcase

Now in a permanent location, Souvenir has a fervent following thanks to the pop-ups previously operated by owner Danielle Suppa. The shop's whitewashed interior is a deliberately blank canvas on which to show products. "We're inspired by Scandinavian and Japanese simplicity, mixed with mid-century modern and Italian influences, and a dash of island and beach culture," says Suppa. "We want to be a place where people can have a conversation about design or ideas." The shop has everything from Akai Ceramic Studio and Stone & Vein stationery to artwork.
1232 College Street, M6H 1C2
souvenir-studios.com

⑥
Blue Button Shop, Little Portugal
Japanese minimalism

Fed up with the lack of quality Japanese goods in North America, Brian Cheuk and Tamae Miyazaki opened a shop to fill the gap. Most of their products are sourced from Japan but the minimalist space has international flair. Industrial clothing racks carry neutral pieces for both men and women, from brands such as Maillot, Engineered Garments and Kapital. Cheuk describes his approach as "slow fashion with a twist". The shop also carries accessories, luggage, toiletries, stationery and homeware.
1499 Dundas Street West, M6K 1T6
+ 1 647 606 3270
bluebuttonshop.com

⑦
Soop Soop, Little Portugal
Fashion and more

In 2014, Christina Pretti and Jordan Puopolo set up the bricks-and-mortar outpost of their online retailer. Their unisex brand is made in Toronto but the shop also carries an eclectic mix of global labels such as Atelier Wonder, Ground Zero, Sunnei and Nattofranco.

"Each season we have a specific colour in mind when buying," says Pretti. The result is a tight edit of pieces that reflect a minimal, youthful aesthetic. Soop Soop also stocks hard-to-find fashion and design periodicals, such as *Another Man*, *Lula*, *Novembre* and *Violet*.
1315 Dundas Street West, M6J 1X8
+ 1 647 748 7667
soopsoop.ca

⑧

The Old Country Shop, Roncesvalles Village
European curios

Sabine Smith's third-generation German immigrant grandfather opened the Old Country Shop – a general store where the then predominantly German community could find items that reminded them of home – in 1961. "We have people who have been coming here since we opened," says Smith, who today runs the shop with her mother and aunt.

The family sources all of the products from Europe, including traditional bier steins, Niederegger marzipan, Darbo jams and hand-painted Russian matryoshka dolls.

The humble shop has endured the vagaries of economic cycles and an ever-changing neighbourhood. In recent years Roncesvalles has grown in popularity with a younger, more diverse crowd and the shop's European flair has found a new receptive audience in them.
355 Roncesvalles Avenue, M6R 2M8
+1 416 535 7641
oldcountryshop.ca

 ⑨

Likely General, Roncesvalles Village
Everything ethical

As its name suggests, this shop stocks a bit of everything, from ceramics and stationery to clothing and accessories. "About 70 per cent of what we carry is Canadian and the rest is international," says Brooke Manning, who opened her shop to showcase ethically produced handmade goods from small-scale producers.

Working in the art and music sectors, she also nurses the neighbourhood's creative scene with regular artisan-run workshops and monthly exhibitions in the cosy gallery space at the rear of the shop.
389 Roncesvalles Avenue, M6R 2N1
+1 647 351 4590

Menswear
Streetwear and more

①

Working Title, Rosedale
Retail meets art

Equal parts menswear boutique, art gallery and bookshop, Working Title challenges the conventions of the run-of-the-mill retail experience. Partners Michael Fong and Paul Shkordoff have positioned the shop as a multi-use art space, regularly hosting exhibitions in collaboration with creatives and makers from around the world. The retail selection is a natural extension of this philosophy. Expect a thoughtful mix of cutting-edge European designers, elevated casualwear and clean basics. It's an expression of the pair's hyper-contemporary yet grounded vision of how art and retail should coexist.
126A Davenport Road, M5R 1H9
+1 416 551 1085
workingtitleshop.com

Fur real
———
Hudson's Bay started out as a fur-trading business in the 17th century. It remains a stalwart in Canadian retail, operating 90 department stores across the country; outposts in Toronto include Bloor and Queen streets. They sell everything from Egyptian cotton bed linen to Birkenstock sandals.
thebay.com

Strict criteria
—
The owners select only well-designed pieces

② Park & Province, Trinity Bellwoods
Niche brands

Chris Naidu and Gray Butler met working in retail and got on so well that they decided to open their own shop. Focusing on easy-to-wear wardrobe staples, the shop carries brands that aren't as well-represented in the fashion-heavy West Queen West neighbourhood. You'll find clothing such as brushed Egyptian cotton shirts from Portuguese Flannel, parkas from Cape Heights in the US and bags from New York's Ernest Alexander.

There's also a patio: it's a nice spot for a pit-stop on the weekends if the nearby park is too busy.
927 Queen Street West, M6J 1G5
+ 1 647 348 3311
parkprovince.com

927   PARK & PROVINCE

Just... one...
more... shop...

③ Klaxon Howl, Trinity Bellwoods
Vintage aesthetic

Toronto designer Matt Robinson's vintage and military-inspired menswear has taken the city by storm in recent years. If you need proof, check out the staff uniforms at the UP Express airport link: they were designed by Robinson and represent his signature aesthetic.

Klaxon Howl is a world away from the exclusive runway shows that Robinson puts on as part of Toronto Fashion Week. It's located in a coach house tucked in an alleyway just off Queen West; the vibe of the shop is cosy and eclectic, with vintage finds hanging alongside Robinson's own pieces. "I make contemporary clothes by pulling details and designs from the past," he says. Drop in for made-to-measure suits, workshirts, boots, leather jackets, casual headwear and more.
694 Queen Street West, M6J 1E7
+ 1 647 436 6628
klaxonhowl.com

Menswear designers

01 Christopher Bates:
Bates trained in Milan's Istituto Marangoni and was chosen to design Air Canada's uniform. His eye for detail is evident in his sharp suits.
christopherbates.com

02 Sydney Mamane:
Mamane's label United Stock Dry Goods' timeless range of denim, shirts and chinos are designed to be wardrobe staples. They can be found in his West Queen West shop.
shopsydneys.com

03 Andrew Coimbra:
A youthful voice in men's fashion, Coimbra incorporates the use of colours and prints in his streetwear.
andrewcoimbra.com

Jonathan + Olivia, Trinity Bellwoods
International hub

A cornerstone of the revitalised Ossington strip, J+O is a fashion retailer with a decidedly west-coast vibe. The shop caters to both men and women and maintains a friendly and open atmosphere.

Jackie O'Brien moved from Vancouver and set up her Toronto shop in 2008. Since then she and her husband have focused on growing her selection of in-demand international designers. Alongside favourites such as Acne Studios, Isabel Marant and Alexander Wang, you'll find a host of more avant-garde pieces from Rick Owens, DRKSHDW and Vetements. It's a necessary stop on any Toronto shopping trip.
49 Ossington Avenue, M6J 2Y9
+1 416 849 5956
jonathanandolivia.com

④
Nomad, West Queen West
Lines on the edge

Though its name might suggest something of a fleeting presence, Nomad has been a mainstay of Toronto's menswear scene for at least a decade.

With a tilt towards high-end streetwear, the shop has carved out a reputation for covetable designer goods that are as impeccably tailored as they are edgy. As well as limited-edition lines from the likes of Fear of God, the shop carries a range of fashion staples such as Gitman Bros, Engineered Garments and Reigning Champ.
819 Queen Street West, M6J 1G1
+1 416 202 8777
nomadshop.net

② Model Citizen, Kensington Market
Up-and-coming designers

What originally began as a small T-shirt screen-printing operation has grown to become an essential spot for clothes by Toronto's emerging designers. Though Model Citizen now carries menswear from around the world, a clear emphasis on homegrown talent remains. Discover new names such as Kollar Clothing, Wordsmiths United and Common-Folk alongside more established labels such as United Stock Dry Goods and Filson.

The screen-printing still occurs in the back and owner Julian Finkel teaches workshops on the craft.
279 Augusta Avenue, M5T 2M1
+1 416 553 6632
modelcitizentoronto.com

③ Philistine, Trinity Bellwoods
Cultured classics

After operating online and as pop-ups around Toronto, Philistine found a permanent home on Queen Street West in 2010. "It all started off with two friends driving down to small towns to collect neat little pieces during our days off," says Colleen Ramage, who co-founded the shop with Aaron Doucet.

Philistine's name belies their painstaking efforts to expand the range while keeping quality tight: besides clothing, customers can find Otter Wax products, Timex watches and a number of independent publications.

As one of the few shops in the city to sell both new and vintage pieces, the layout reflects the marriage of old and new. Antique fixtures include a 1940s radio cabinet and a classic wood-canvas canoe repurposed to display seasonal pieces.
928 Queen Street West, M6J 1G6
+1 416 532 3662
philistinetoronto.com

①
Pink Tartan, Yorkville
Global range

Housed in a two-storey building
from 1837, Pink Tartan's flagship
showcases "preppy chic" staples.
Designer and owner Kimberley
Newport-Mimran has also brought
in clothing and accessories from
brands such as Montréal's Want
Les Essentiels, English footwear
designer Paul Andrew and Totême
in New York. There's a mix of other
items, including Japanese paper-
covered tea tins, Mrs John L Strong
stationery and Binchotan charcoal
toothbrushes. A selection of art
from Newport-Mimran's personal
collection adorns the walls.
77 Yorkville Avenue, M5R 1C1
+1 416 967 7700
pinktartan.com

②
119 Corbo, Yorkville
Beautiful lines

With its dark-wood finishings and
colour-coordinated ensembles, 119
Corbo is not unlike a glamorous
walk-in wardrobe. Everything is
hand-picked by owner Linda Perisa,
whose penchant for clean lines and
muted tones is evident in her stock.
"We want to reinforce how beautiful
things should be treated," she says.
 Designers such as the Antwerp
Six's Ann Demeulemeester and
Colombia's Haider Ackermann
made their first foray into Canada
here. You'll also be able to find
Perisa's own leather, jersey and
cashmere creations.
119 Yorkville Avenue, M5R 1C4
+1 416 928 0954
119corbo.com

③
Ewanika, The Annex
Simple sophistication

Trish Ewanika has quietly
established her eponymous
boutique as a destination for a
sharp selection of womenswear.
Whether it's Barena Venezia or
Samuji, each of the 40 or so global
brands has been carefully chosen
in line with Ewanika's penchant
for soft natural fabrics.
 Her own designs have a simple
functionality, classic lines and
muted colours. "We balance ease
of sophistication with clarity," she
says. Also available are accessories
to pair with the clothing, including
handbags, hats and jewellery.
1083 Bathurst Street, M5R 3G8
+1 416 927 9699
ewanika.ca

④
Hoi Bo, Distillery District
Handmade gems

Started in 2007 by Sarra Tang,
Hoi Bo has become synonymous
with refined design in Toronto.
The brand began with waxed
canvas bags and has since expanded
into clothing and jewellery.

Everything here is handmade
by Tang and her team of eight.
With a keen eye for aesthetics
and an unwavering commitment
to function, she has carved out
a unique niche using natural
materials that are not only
beautiful but age well too.

She cites her goal as being able
to create pieces that are accessible
to everyone regardless of their
size, shape, age or gender. "I'm
inspired by the process," says
Tang, whose voluminous tunics of
Belgian linen and dry-wax bags
made using pure Ontario beeswax
are evidence of her commitment
to the cause.
15 Trinity Street, M5A 3C4
+1 647 852 5488
hoibo.com

⑤
The Narwhal, Summerhill
Small but wide-ranging

Tucked away in Toronto's
Summerhill neighbourhood,
multibrand womenswear
retailer The Narwhal feels like
a hidden gem. Though small,
the warm and inviting space
offers a wide variety of highly
versatile pieces. Opened in 2010
by Sydney Wills and Marisa
Buchowsky, the shop carries
international labels including
Ulla Johnson, Apiece Apart,
Acne Studios, Rachel Comey
and Common Projects.

With backgrounds in interior
design and retail the owners share
a distinct eye for accessible fashion,
which has attracted a diverse and
devoted clientele. Buchowsky says
she wants to sell clothes that
are "wearable but a little bit
outside the box". There is also
a small selection of delicate
jewellery and bold accessories.
8 Price Street, M4W 1Z4
+1 647 351 5011
narwhalboutique.com

Homeware
House specials

①
Bungalow, Kensington Market
Past presence

You'll likely be drawn in by the beautiful furniture on display in the front window, but Kensington Market's Bungalow also stocks a great selection of new and vintage clothing and jewellery. Along with the usual suspects such as Herschel and Obey, owners Paul Salsman and Jessica Zimmermann also stock screen-printed T-shirts and jewellery sourced from One of a Kind Show (a marketplace for local makers).

In the back are racks of vintage clothing but the real goldmine is in the basement where there are two rooms of mid-century modern furniture, including couches, kitchen tables and chairs. If you want to outfit your apartment to look like a set from *Mad Men*, Bungalow has you covered.
273 Augusta Avenue, M5T 2M1
+1 416 598 0204
bungalow.to

②
Mjölk, The Junction
Creative partnerships

Scandinavia meets Japan at Mjölk (pronounced "mi-yelk"; it's Swedish for "milk"). With a focus on high-end design and clean aesthetics, it's a labour of love for married couple John Baker and Juli Daoust (*both pictured*). Their meticulous selection of pieces ranges from classic Danish furniture by Finn Juhl to beautifully crafted houseware from Oji Masanori. The couple partner with their favourite designers to develop products that espouse their vision of impeccable craftsmanship, documenting the collaborations in a self-published magazine series.
2959 Dundas Street West, M6P 1Z2
+1 416 551 9853
mjolk.ca

(1)
Soundscapes, Little Italy
Worth a listen

This record shop's O-shaped logo was inspired by owner Greg Davis's favourite album: *Ladies & Gentlemen, we are Floating in Space* by English rock band Spiritualized. "The store is dedicated to carrying the best music of all genres, to help people discover music that wasn't necessarily popular but definitely worthy of discovery," he says. Even in today's Spotify age, many still come to Soundscapes to hunt out new music the traditional way: by flipping through record sleeves and asking shop staff for recommendations. Besides records Soundscapes also sells CDs, music DVDs, books, magazines and concert tickets.
572 College Street, M6G 1B3
+1 416 537 1620
soundscapesmusic.com

(3)
Avenue Road, Leslieville
Eclectic Avenue

This massive, lofty showroom space, once home to the printing facilities of a local Chinese newspaper, now holds Avenue Road's collection of refined furniture and home decor. All three floors of exhibition space are open to the public and provide a rare opportunity to view fine furnishings designed by international names such as Oscar Niemeyer, Christophe Delcourt and Bruno Moinard.
415 Eastern Avenue, M4M 1B7
+1 416 548 7788
avenue-road.com

(2)
June Records, Little Italy
Sound advice

This sprightly record shop sells a well-rounded collection of new and vintage vinyl. Staff are attentive and always on hand to suggest an album based on your musical proclivities. Chances are you'll find yourself leaving with more than one unexpected find.
662 College Street, M6G 1B8
+1 416 516 5863
junerecords.com

Ah, my favourite Canadian song: Celine Dion's 'Fly'... doo doo...

③
Cosmos, West Queen West
Out of this world

Aki Abe (*pictured bottom, on right*) opened one of the city's first all-vinyl shops in 1998. He currently has two outposts on Queen Street West: Cosmos Records focuses on rock and soul music while Cosmos West Records is a jazz and funk collector's dream. Both locations deal exclusively in original vinyl and everything is hand-picked by Abe himself. Ask for a recommendation and see where he takes you.
Cosmos Records:
607A Queen Street West, M5V 2B7
+1 416 603 0254
Cosmos West Records:
652 Queen Street West, M6J 1E5
+1 416 861 9228
cosmosrecords.ca

④
Quixotic Sounds, Little Italy
Tale of two cities

Eleven years after opening a record shop in Vevey, Switzerland in 2004, Swiss native Pascal Roth set up a sister location in Toronto. "The idea behind the two stores is to offer customers on two different continents access to records that are pretty rare on the other side," says Roth.

The spacious shop is outfitted with a coffee bar and a piano, making it the perfect stage for the musical gigs by homegrown acts that are hosted here every month.
938 College Street, M6H 1A4
+1 647 345 9195

In a spin

Feeling inspired after attending a concert and need to get your hands on the band's vinyl right away? Try Grasshopper Records in Trinity Bellwoods. The shop carries an eclectic range and is open every evening until midnight.
grasshopperrecords.ca

Sonic Boom, Chinatown
Vinyl destination

Once located in the historic
department store Honest Ed's,
Sonic Boom is Canada's biggest
independent record store and has
the largest collection of vinyl in the
country (it also has a great selection
of music on cassette). The staff are all
experts, with some having been with
the shop for more than a decade.

It also stocks products such as
record players, band T-shirts, beer-
making kits and a wall of sweets.
Of note is the section of music
books and graphic novels, plus a
large selection of Choose Your Own
Adventure novels.
215 Spadina Avenue, M5T 2C7
+1 416 532 0334
sonicboommusic.com

① Brika, Leslieville
Neighbourhood favourite

New Jersey's Jen Lee Koss established her company Brika with Newfoundlander Kena Paranjape in 2012, initially as an online marketplace selling small-batch products by artisans and craftsmen from across the US and Canada. The duo opened their first bricks-and-mortar space in 2015, followed by this second location in Leslieville in the summer of 2016. "We want to be everyone's neighbourhood shop," says Koss.

Brika works with designers on exclusive collaborations so you're bound to find something special and unique. Little placards are placed alongside the scented candles, tea towels and other items to introduce customers to the makers behind them.
768 Queen Street East M4M 1H4
+1 844 472 7452
brika.com

I enjoy a smart, season-appropriate jumper

② BYOB Cocktail Emporium, Trinity Bellwoods
Shake it till you make it

Toronto's first and only cocktail shop takes an all-encompassing approach to the craft, carrying everything from recipe books and Japanese bar tools to absinthe fountains and vintage glassware. "BYOB has a large range of products sourced from around the globe," says founder Kristen Voisey. "We're a one-stop shop for all beginners looking to set up home bars."

Besides selling all the equipment you could ever need, BYOB is home to the largest collection of cocktail ingredients in North America, with more than 200 different types of bitters from around the world. A sister shop, sporting a Miami-pink exterior and vintage gold shelving units to match its eclectic selection, was launched in Kensington Market in 2015.
972 Queen Street West, M6J 1H1
+1 647 727 3600
cocktailemporium.ca

Blurring the lines between retailer and workshop, Kid Icarus allows visitors to observe the screen-printing process while they shop. In addition to the studio's own line of greeting cards, posters and colouring books, the shop sells a good range of arts-and-crafts supplies.
205 Augusta Avenue, M5T 2L4
+1 416 977 7236
kidicarus.ca

⑤
Want Apothecary, Rosedale
Form and function

Want Apothecary was co-founded by twins Byron and Dexter Peart, the designers behind Montréal-based accessories brand Want Les Essentiels. "Our products and solutions will always respond to the modern traveller's needs," says Byron. "We strive to create beautiful yet functional products that are essential, purposeful and made to last," adds Dexter.

The shop also presents a sharp edit of international fashion brands such as Acne Studios, Filippa K, Comme des Garçons and Junya Watanabe.
1070 Yonge Street, M4W 3V7
+1 416 924 8080
wantapothecary.com

③
The Paper Place, Trinity Bellwoods
Items of note

If you're the kind of person who compulsively buys fresh notebooks to jot your ideas in, The Paper Place, right next door to popular bookshop Type (*see page 69*), is the perfect spot to fuel your addiction. In addition to the ubiquitous line of Moleskine products and notebooks from lesser-known brands, there's a large selection of novelty stationery products (think cat-shaped erasers and what must be the world's tiniest set of coloured pencils), envelopes, ribbons and stamps.

The Paper Place also carries more than 2,000 different kinds of paper from Japan, Nepal, Brazil, Italy, Germany and the rest of the world. While the selection is overwhelming, owner Heather Sauer has a clear favourite: "the gorgeous stencil-dyed Katazome papers from Japan".
887 Queen Street West, M6J 1G5
+1 416 703 0089
thepaperplace.ca

Shopping malls

If you're looking for a convenient place to do a spot of shopping, Toronto has some of the best malls around thanks to companies such as Cadillac Fairview and Oxford Properties, which have based their HQs here. Both firms have also set the global standard for shopping centres in cities such as London and Rio. Here's a round-up of our favourite Toronto picks.

01 Yorkdale, Lawrence Heights: This high-end shopping mall on the northern tip of Toronto draws in many of the city's most discerning shoppers. It's where companies such as Burberry have chosen to introduce their brands to the domestic market.
yorkdale.com

02 Sherway Gardens, Etobicoke: If you've arrived at Toronto Pearson International Airport and only have a few hours to spare for a spot of shopping, Sherway Gardens is a convenient option. Just a 10-minute drive from the airport, this shopping centre underwent an expansion in 2015 to accomodate 50 new shops.
cfshops.com/sherway-gardens.html

03 Toronto Eaton Centre, Yonge-Dundas: This eye-catching shopping centre at the heart of Downtown is bookended by Dundas and Queen subway stations. Designed by Eberhard Zeidler in 1977, its long glassy skylight infuses the interiors and its 200 shops with natural light.
cfshops.com/toronto-eaton-centre.html

⑥
Knife, Trinity Bellwoods
Cutting edge

"As a Japanese-knife addict, there wasn't a good enough knife shop in Toronto and I knew that we needed one," says Eugene Ong, who quit his cooking job to start his retail business in 2010. The space carries scores of blades made by more than 15 skilled blacksmiths from across Japan, including Mcusta Zanmai, Takeshi Saji and Yu Kurosaki. It also hosts weekly two-hour knife-sharpening classes led by Ong.
249 Crawford Street, M6J 2V7
+1 647 996 8609
knifetoronto.com

⑦
Gravitypope, West Queen West
Wear in the world

Gravitypope's rather unremarkable decor belies its expansive range of brands from Canada and around the world. It's the brainchild of Edmonton-born Louise Dirks, who has filled the shop with clothes, footwear and fashion accessories from English designer Margaret Howell, alongside Italian brands Forte Forte and Marni. Dirks fostered an affinity for international clothing working at an import shop, which saw her travelling the world in search of items from Morocco, Turkey, Guatemala, India and Nepal.
1010 Queen Street West, M6J 1H6
+1 647 748 5155
gravitypope.com

⑧
Wonder Pens, Leslieville
The write tools

Located a little off the beaten track, this lovely stationery shop is housed in a converted factory in Toronto's east end. Inside you'll find a range of notebooks from brands such as Field Notes and Japanese paper company Life. However, the shop's speciality is fountain pens and ink, with exclusive products such as Franklin Christof pens and Noodler's raven black ink. Owners Liz and Jon Chan live behind the shop so you might come across their child playing hide-and-seek around the place.
250 Carlaw Street, M4M 3L1
+1 416 799 5935
wonderpens.ca

Vintage wares
Oldies but goodies

①

Rec & Art History and Weekend Variety, West Queen West
Collectable heaven

Gallerist Katharine Mulherin launched antiques shop Rec & Art History with friend Ron Fraser, a veteran dealer of repurposed home furnishings and collectables. It proved a hit with Toronto's collectors, so when the furnace next door broke down and the tenants vacated, Mulherin decided to expand. "It was kind of a happy accident; suddenly an extra space was available," she says. The result is Weekend Variety, a general shop selling items such as sea-salt soaps, Paine's candles, towels, blankets and Turkish tea.
1080 Queen Street West, M6J 1H8
+ 1 416 993 6510

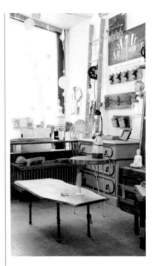

②

Arts Market, Leslieville
Creative hub

Before launching Arts Market in 2011, Daniel Cohen spent six years creating and selling his own artwork in outdoor markets in cities including Sydney, Seoul, Buenos Aires and Bangkok. "When I moved back to Toronto I was looking for something similar but was unable to find it – so I decided to open a suitable option," he says.

Cohen first opened leasing spaces to creatives interested in honing their brands, meeting other artists and selling their work. "We choose people based on product and personality," he says. The market carries hand-crafted items by about 175 Toronto artisans, from cards and jewellery to portraits and industrial lighting. Today Arts Market remains at the centre of Toronto's artistic community with three different citywide outposts.
1114 Queen Street East, M4M 1K7
+ 1 647 997 7616
artsmarket.ca

Inside info
—
The shop posts new pieces on its blog

What? I don't want to miss the Maple Leafs game

①
The Monkey's Paw, Junction
Triangle
Literary treasure hunt

You won't come across the latest
Stephen King novel at The Monkey's
Paw but you might find something
that could have inspired it: the
shelves, which are unlabelled to
encourage browsing and surprise
finds, are filled with rare titles
alongside odd curiosities like a
selection of beetles encased in Lucite.

Not to be missed is the custom-
built Biblio-Mat, which owner Stephen
Fowler (*pictured*) calls "the world's
only antiquarian book-randomising
vending machine". Drop a CA$2
coin into the Biblio-Mat and receive
a rare treasure. The machine has
become so popular that Fowler now
sources books specifically for it.
1267 Bloor Street West, M6H 1N7
+1 416 531 2123
monkeyspaw.com

③
Queen West Antique Centre,
West Queen West
Far-flung finds

Amy Mason established Queen
West Antique Centre in 1997,
bringing years of experience from
participating in antique shows. She
and her husband travel more than
100,000km annually to keep the
showroom stocked with interesting
pieces. "We do our best to ensure
all items in the store are authentic
original designs – no shoddy
replicas or reproductions," she says.
Bestselling items include the Lotte
lamps created by Danish immigrants
Lotte and Gunnar Bostlund in
Canada in the late 1950s.
1605 Queen Street West, M6R 1A9
+1 416 588 2212
qwac.ca

②
Balfour Books, Little Italy
Pre-loved pages

This second-hand bookshop is a
College Street institution. Owner
Joyce Blair (*pictured*) has built
up an expansive selection of art,
fashion, film, photography and
architecture books, along with a
broad range of fiction. If you're
after something a little more
compact, the centre of the shop
floor contains a double-sided
rack filled with pocket books that
include many classic titles. The
more popular titles are stacked
towards the back of the shop.
468 College Street, M6G 1A1
+1 416 531 9911
balfourbooks.squarespace.com

③
Swipe Design, Chinatown
Swipe right

This is a book and gift shop that caters to Toronto's design aficionados. "You could call us a one-stop shop for designers, architects and those with an interest in design," says manager Kellie Hadjidimitriou.

It carries design classics such as Alvar Aalto's Savoy Vase and Chemex coffee makers. "It has to look good but more importantly, it has to work well," says Hadjidimitriou of how she chooses what products to stock.

B04, 401 Richmond Street West, M5V 3A8
+ 1 416 363 1332
swipe.com

Community hub
—
Glad Day has become a symbol of the city's progressive values. Founded in 1970, it is the world's oldest bookshop in operation targeted at the LGBT community. It also hosts readings, art shows and social meetings.
gladdaybookshop.com

④
Ben McNally, Financial District
Tightly edited

Bay Street in Toronto's Financial District may seem an odd place for an old-school bookshop but Ben McNally has found success here. He says his establishment – a tidy, reserved environment infused with warm light and accented by dark-wood finishings – is characterised as much by what's not in it as what is. Forgoing the usual knick-knacks and magazines you find in bookshops, it's a business that reveres and revolves around the book. History and biography tomes feature prominently.
366 Bay Street, M5H 4B2
+ 1 416 361 0032
benmcnallybooks.com

⑤
Indigo Books, Etobicoke
Temple of print

Twenty years after its founding, Indigo Books opened a new two-storey concept in Sherway Gardens shopping centre (*see page 64*) in 2016. Designed by Diego Burdi, the bookshelves and drywalls have been angled to draw the eye to the well-appointed nooks and crannies. "We've created a bookshop that's also a meeting space," says Burdi. "Bookshops need to offer more than just books."

"Any format needs to be reimagined," adds CEO Heather Reisman. "I love the opportunity to meander and find surprises."
25 The West Mall, M9C 1B8
+ 1 416 622 3769
chapters.indigo.ca

Lost the plot
—
The shop has a section for "plotless fiction"

 6

Type, Trinity Bellwoods
Tome capsule

Established in 2006 across from Trinity Bellwoods Park on Queen Street West, Type Books is one of the city's most beloved indie bookshops. It has a warm living-room feel and the shop's friendly staff – many of them writers and artists – are accessible and helpful. Type is "a store built for browsing", says staff member Derek McCormack. "The general rule of the store is: order the titles that customers can't find at big bookstores or at airports."

Indeed, the thoughtfully edited shelves are jam-packed with interesting and unusual finds while the display tables in the centre are always filled with gems, including books by Toronto's very own wordsmiths. There's also a lovely children's section tucked away at the back.
883 Queen Street West, M6J 1G5
+1 416 366 8973
typebooks.ca

Things we'd buy
—— Toronto take-homes

If you're planning a visit to Toronto, it may be wise to bring an extra suitcase. A quick jaunt around the city's retail offerings will provide you with more than enough temptation to fill it.

As with everything else about the city, diversity is the name of the game. Toronto's creatives are as many and varied as its populace, so you're sure to pick up something you're unlikely to find anywhere else in the world. From a conversation-starting Mountie thermos by Drake General Store and quirky printed items from Kid Icarus to quality fashion basics from Kotn and craft beer by Bellwoods Brewery, there's plenty here to give your wallet a workout.

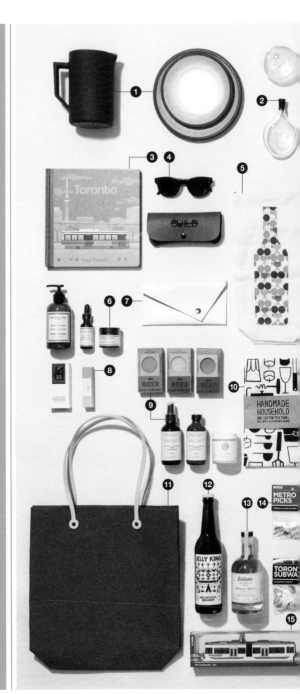

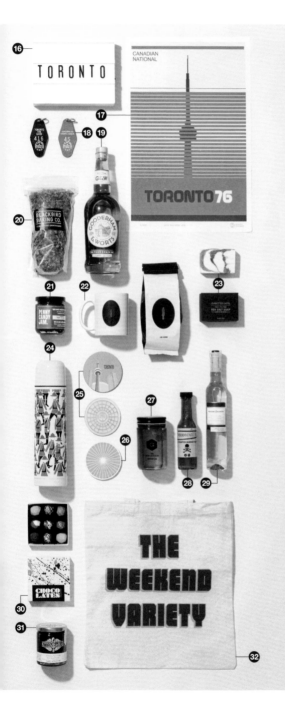

01 Tableware by Herriott Grace
herriottgrace.com
02 Goodbeast vase and flask
from Easy Tiger
easytigergoods.com
03 *Toronto ABC* book from
Spacing *spacingstore.ca*
04 Guild sunglasses from
Spacing *spacingstore.ca*
05 Wine bag by Tiff *tiff.net*
06 Skincare by Crawford Street
crawfordskincare.com
07 Eek handmade wallet from
Likely General
likelygeneral.tumblr.com
08 Fragrances from Souvenir
souvenir-studios.com
09 Skincare from Likely General
likelygeneral.tumblr.com
10 Paul Dotey teatowel from
Kid Icarus *kidicarus.ca*
11 Shopper tote by Hoi Bo
hoibo.com
12 Beer by Bellwoods Brewery
bellwoodsbrewery.com
13 Dillon's Distillers rose gin
from Easy Tiger
easytigergoods.com
14 Metro guitar picks and
Toronto subway badges from
Spacing *spacingstore.ca*
15 TTC Streetcar from Spacing
spacingstore.ca
16 Lightbox by Tiff *tiff.net*
17 Toronto 76 print from
Spacing *spacingstore.ca*
18 Keyrings from Spacing
spacingstore.ca
19 Gooderham & Worts
whiskey from LCBO *lcbo.com*
20 Granola by Blackbird Baking
Co *blackbirdbakingco.com*
21 Penny Candy jam from The
Lucky Penny *+1 416 516 9666*
22 Cut coffee mug and coffee
beans from Sam James Coffee
Bar *samjamescoffeebar.com*
23 Charlotte & Castel soap
from Souvenir
souvenir-studios.com
24 Mountie thermos by Drake
General Store
drakegeneralstore.ca
25 Coasters from Spacing
spacingstore.ca
26 Xenia Taler coaster from
Souvenir
souvenir-studios.com
27 Gibbs honey from
Easy Tiger
easytigergoods.com

28 Hot sauce from The Lucky
Penny *+1 416 516 9666*
29 Ice-wine from Pearl
Morissette *pearlmorissette.com*
30 Chocolates by Brandon
Olsen *cxbo.ca*
31 Jam by Kitten & the Bear
kittenandthebear.com
32 Tote by The Weekend Variety
+1 416 993 6510
33 T-shirt from Kotn *kotn.com*
34 Arborist sweatshirt from

Drake General Store
drakegeneralstore.ca
35 Toronto Blue Jays T-shirt
from Drake General Store
drakegeneralstore.ca
36 Womenswear by Hoi Bo
hoibo.com
37 M James pocket square
from Souvenir
souvenir-studios.com
38 Backpack by YNOT
ynotmade.com

39 Shared baby's blanket from
Drake General Store
drakegeneralstore.ca
40 Darzé trainers from
Working Title
workingtitleshop.com
41 Rug by Likely General
+1 647 351 4590
42 The Weeknd album from
June Records
junerecords.com

12 essays
— Defining Toronto

1
Identity crisis
Toronto's changing image
by Christopher Frey,
writer

2
Lady of the lake
Pioneering swimmer
by Marilyn Bell DiLascio,
former long-distance
swimmer

3
The not-quite
breakfast club
Toronto's signature meal
by Jason Li,
Monocle

4
The Frankenstein effect
Toronto's built form
by Alex Bozikovic,
writer

5
Crisis talks
Community spirit
by Tomos Lewis,
Monocle

6
Get your skates on
Home of hockey
by Dani Couture,
writer

7
Built-up area
Defining the population
by Cameron Bailey,
Creative director of the
Toronto International
Film Festival

8
The more things change...
Torontonian values
by John Tory,
Mayor of Toronto

9
Wander woman
Jane's walk
by Denise Pinto,
landscape architect

10
Mixed portfolio
Entrepreneurial Toronto
by Tim Draimin,
social innovator

11
Sing when you're winning
The Four Seasons Centre
by Sarah Fulford,
writer and editor

12
Having your cake,
not eating it
The fall and legacy
of Rob Ford
by Jennifer Pagliaro,
journalist

When I said I wanted to 'curl up' I meant on a sofa with this essay section!

ESSAY 01

Identity crisis
Toronto's changing image

Unlike London, Paris or New York, Toronto seems not to have a well-defined identity. For its inhabitants, however, this is probably a good thing.

by Christopher Frey, writer

Whenever I go on bike rides to Toronto's east end, I usually take the Queen Street Viaduct across the Don River. It was built in 1911 but if the single-span, steel truss bridge is notable for its historical value, that's only because the city is relatively young. What really draws me to the bridge is the public art that was installed much later on its west-facing portal. It's a stainless steel cut-out of the words, "This river I step in is not the river I stand in," accompanied by a backless clock with an outer ring that glows at night.

The piece by artist Eldon Garnet riffs on a phrase from Heraclitus about the transient nature of time. But there's something about its urban context that gives the words a parallel meaning for me.

The bridge connects two rapidly gentrifying neighbourhoods; the river it spans was one of the city's first industrial settings and is now in the midst of long-term remediation. So for me, the appeal of the artwork's phrase is in the way it articulates our relationship to urban centres – how a city is forever a work in progress. This is especially palpable in Toronto.

To take visual measure of those changes I need only ride a few more minutes south to Corktown Common, a recently created park built atop a former brownfield site. Here, lush wetland ponds and fields of prairie grass encircle a bank designed to protect against flooding from the Don River. But the bank itself, topped with a smart-looking pavilion and splash pads, also offers one of my favourite panoramas of the city's restless, ever-changing skyline.

In the foreground a covey of attractively modernist mid-rises, first opened to serve as the athlete's village for the 2015 Pan Am Games, is coming to life as the planned, mixed-income community of Canary District. Further on the signature pieces of Toronto's skyline – the CN Tower, the Toronto-Dominion Centre, First Canadian Place – compete for attention with a host of office towers and clustered condos. Toronto boasts the second-most high-rises among North American cities (behind only New York) and Corktown Common would be as good a place as any to capture this development unfolding with time-lapse photography. But taking in the view from here sometimes has the side effect of making me feel old; blink and a new neighbourhood has gone up.

But big buildings only tell one part of the story of how the city is changing. With more than 100,000 new arrivals every year, it's the demographic of who is living and working inside those buildings that give Toronto's story even greater significance.

"We're still trying to figure out how to even talk about this emerging city"

The Toronto I knew growing up in the 1970s and 1980s was multicultural – but not yet cosmopolitan. Until the 1960s more than 80 per cent of immigrants were European. But changes to immigration policy ushered in newcomers from the Caribbean, China, South Asia and Latin America, helping Toronto to surpass Montréal not just as Canada's biggest city but also as its cultural and financial capital. It just took a little more time for the city to finally outgrow the Anglo-Protestant provincialism that once earned it the moniker of "New York as run by the Swiss".

All cities are a work in progress, forever remaking themselves, layering new history over the old. But some more than others; young, ascendant cities such as Toronto that are just now experiencing their defining period of prominence and growth. And not just physically but also in the imagination: the stories people tell about them and the way they are talked about from afar (if they are talked about at all).

Whatever ideas or images we already carry in our heads about London, Tokyo, Paris and Moscow aren't likely to change very much. Augmented by the personal experience we may have with those cities, they are largely fixed in our imagination. The fact that Toronto doesn't have much of an established identity, ethnic, historical or otherwise, is what ideally gives all newcomers a say in its making. Reading local newspapers and magazines, one gets the sense that we're still trying to figure out how to even talk about this emerging city, as though it's in the midst of a paradigm shift and the old clichés and categories no longer apply.

While many of Toronto's novelists and short-story writers have made the city their subject, chronicling its essentially immigrant character, its profile in pop culture is more tenuous. With their city a leading hub for film and television production in North America, Torontonians long ago got used to the idea of their city as a stand-in for some other place – typically New York or Chicago.

We've built an entire creative industry around pretending to be somewhere else, providing the set for American stories told to a global audience. Which is why Rob Ford's recent, headline-grabbing term as mayor may have been one of the best things to have ever happened to the city. On policy and governance, Ford was a disaster. But he did give us a personality of Shakespearean proportions, equal parts Falstaff and Prince Hal. Through Ford, Toronto finally got to play itself. — (M)

ESSAY 02

Lady of the lake
Pioneering swimmer
—

Prior to 1954, no one had ever swum across Lake Ontario. Then a 16-year-old girl agreed to race the most famous US swimmer of the day to the farthest shore.

*by Marilyn Bell DiLascio,
former long-distance
swimmer*

I have always described my life as being in two parts: before I swam Lake Ontario and after I swam Lake Ontario. Because life was never the same after that.

It was just before 23.15 on 8 September 1954. No one had ever swum across the lake before. I was 16 years old and had never attempted to swim in the dark.

It had been stormy all day and it was still raining; there was no moon, there were no stars. It was overcast, rainy and very rough.

I began my swim at the coastguard station in Youngstown on the New York state side of the Niagara River, which feeds into the lake. My coach Gus Ryder couldn't get his boat to the starting point, so he told me, "Just dive into the water and swim out. Get out into the middle of the channel and just swim straight. I will find you." I was scared but I believed him.

I was wearing a black nylon bathing suit and a pair of very old goggles. They

ABOUT THE WRITER: Christopher Frey is Monocle's Toronto correspondent and the founding editor of *Hazlitt* magazine. His forthcoming book, *Broken Atlas*, chronicles the past 10 years of globalisation.

were enormous and looked like something a miner would wear underground. I ditched them after a couple of hours because they gave me such a terrible headache, so I swam most of the way without them.

I dived into the water and started to swim. I was petrified. I immediately felt lost. The sky was pitch black, I couldn't see the horizon and there was nothing in the distance for me to focus on. It was just all black; the water was black, the sky was black. Then, after about half an hour, I heard Gus's voice calling my name from the boat. He had found me. I was so relieved.

"I was petrified. I immediately felt lost. The sky was pitch black, I couldn't see the horizon"

Gus had been my coach since I was 11 years old. My family had moved back to Toronto in 1946 after the Second World War, following my dad's posting in Nova Scotia. For the first six months, we lived at the Royal York Hotel because housing in the city was so scarce.

This is when I remember going to Lake Ontario for the first time. I used to take the streetcar down to the shore from the hotel on Front Street and take the ferry to Toronto Island, where we'd swim, have picnics and go on the rides at the amusement park. Those were wonderful days.

Gus used to say that I wasn't a very fast swimmer but that I could swim forever. I think that's what gave him the idea for the swim across the lake. I swam my first mile when I was 11 and began training in earnest for long distances when I was 12. My training was quite primitive back then: it was just swimming, swimming, swimming, for about three-and-a-half hours every day.

My first long-distance race came in June 1954: the world championships in Atlantic City. The race was 26 miles [42km] long and I finished ninth. I was the first woman to complete the race. For that year's Canadian National

Exhibition the organisers invited Florence Chadwick, the most famous American swimmer of her day, to attempt the swim across Lake Ontario. They offered her a reward of $10,000 if she completed the swim. This infuriated lots of the open-water swimmers in America and Canada; given that no one had attempted the swim before they felt that it should be a race.

I have no idea what took place behind the scenes but one day Gus came to me and my parents and asked if I wanted to race Florence Chadwick across the lake if we could find a sponsor to cover the costs. *The Toronto Star* agreed to sponsor us and my parents agreed to the race, as long as Gus could guarantee that I'd be safe. Winnie Roach, the first Canadian to swim the English Channel also stepped up to challenge Chadwick, so it was up to us to swim for Canada across Lake Ontario.

That night, Florence began the swim about 20 minutes before me and Winnie followed me a few minutes later. Some time before dawn, both women were pulled out of the race but I didn't know this; nobody told me. I was swimming without any competitors.

Because it was so dark, Gus had a torch that he shone on the water just ahead of my stroke. He shouted to me, "Just swim for the light, don't keep looking up, just swim for the light, that's all you have to do." And that's what I did.

The unfortunate thing is, the eels that live in the lake are attracted to light, so they found the flashlight and they found

Three Toronto sporting stars
—
01 Barbara-Ann Scott
One of the world's best figure-skaters.
02 Penny Oleksiak
2016 Rio Olympics gold-medal-winning swimming star.
03 Andre De Grasse
Rising star of international athletics.

me too. It wasn't pleasant. They were winding and slithering around any limb they could get their teeth into.

I did a lot of stopping. I was really sleep-deprived. I had been awake since five that morning and hadn't slept well the days before. I actually fell asleep in the water a few times. It becomes so mechanical that your body just knows, even when your mind is shutting down, what it has to do.

I saw my first sunrise that day. I'd never been awake that early before. I remember seeing these swatches of light streaking across the sky. My gosh, it was just magnificent. I swam out of the night and into the daylight, and then into the night again.

I don't really remember finishing the swim but I arrived at Toronto's shoreline just under 21 hours after I'd started out, at the other edge of the lake. I found out later that the newspapers in Toronto had been publishing special editions throughout the day, and that the radio stations were broadcasting hourly updates of my progress.

There was a tremendous crowd there and a lot of noise. People were letting off fireworks. It was pandemonium! Some were jumping into the water trying to grab me. When we got to the harbour wall, Gus pulled me into the boat. I couldn't believe it. I was so exhausted but I was thrilled and just so happy that I'd made it.

Lake Ontario is like my lifeblood, still. My whole life has been about the water. The Great Lakes are these fantastic, amazingly beautiful entities between Canada and the US, and it's my dream to make sure that their waters stay clean for the generations that come after me, like they were when I swam across Lake Ontario. — (M)

ABOUT THE WRITER: Marilyn Bell DiLascio was the first person to swim Lake Ontario. In 1955, she became the youngest to swim the English Channel. She lives in New York state and is an advocate and ambassador for Lake Ontario Waterkeeper.

ESSAY 03

The not-quite breakfast club
Toronto's signature meal

On any given weekend morning you'll find Torontonians gathering for brunch, a meal that perfectly encapsulates the city and the attitudes of its inhabitants.

by Jason Li, Monocle

On a recent sunny Sunday morning, a few colleagues and I were at The Federal (*see page 36*) having brunch; a monthly ritual. The proceedings are pretty fixed: we typically meet on Saturday at 10.30 at one of our three go-to restaurants (10.00 would be too early, 11.00 too late; no one wants to begin their weekend queuing for 20 minutes); we order the same dishes, plus bottomless coffee; and when the food arrives, spend the first minutes waxing lyrical about how delicious everything is. With the formalities out of the way we start catching up on each other's lives for the next hour or so before dispersing for the weekend.

Something, however, felt amiss that day. We had known that one of the spots on our roster, Me & Mine, was closing and had planned our weekend around their last brunch service. Scheduling conflicts pushed our meet-up back to Sunday but when we arrived we were greeted by a cold, metallic sign: "CLOSED".

Employees in the sector made up the biggest portion of new immigrants under the government's Express Entry scheme in 2015.

Furthermore, the adage "You are what you eat" holds true for cities. New York and London owe their economic powerhouse status to more than a couple of high-profile lunch spots, while the convivial atmosphere in places such as Seville or Rio de Janeiro is most clearly articulated in its restaurants and watering holes, from the *bodegas* serving tasty tapas suppers to an ice-cold beer near Copacabana at the end of a long day. And if cities are defined by a single meal, Toronto's is, without a doubt, defined by this one. This is why, when a cherished brunch spot closes, there is a genuine sense of loss.

"Brunch is the social glue that holds together this society of many different parts"

As it turned out, their final brunch had been on the previous day. Plans torn asunder, we hastily settled for The Federal, the nearest option.

As we sat around our plates of crispy bacon, poached eggs and sautéed kale, we couldn't help but be distracted by memories of Me & Mine's grilled pork belly and fried chicken benedict, or by its homemade ketchup and beetroot butter. Not even The Federal's delicious Caesars could cheer us up.

Before you think I'm being melodramatic, hear me out. Weekend brunch is the ideal meal for Torontonians, who are not so industrious as to wake up in time for breakfast, nor so lazy as to sleep through lunch. Somewhere between 10.00 to 12.00 is an ideal window. And what's more, weekend brunch is the perfect reflection of the city. It is unfettered by the conventions that plague breakfast, lunch or dinner. Pancakes with berries? Or maybe something savoury, like fried chicken drizzled with something sweet (maple syrup, of course)? Perhaps the healthier option of granola or yoghurt parfait? All legitimate and respectable options.

In much the same way, Toronto is unconcerned by boundaries: there are endless permutations to life in the city and brunch is the social glue that holds together this society of many different parts.

Statistics also reveal that Canada's food and hospitality scene fuels its economy as much as its people.

But, thankfully, new spots pop up all the time. Indeed, for every establishment that pulls down its shutters for good, it seems there are two new ones throwing open their doors.

After we say our goodbyes, I decide there's time to take a walk around. Not two blocks away, I happen across another sign. This one marks the arrival of a new farm-to-table restaurant and guess what? It serves brunch. — (M)

ABOUT THE WRITER: MONOCLE's deputy bureau chief in Toronto, Jason Li transitioned from occasional brunchgoer to zealous advocate when he moved to the city nearly a decade ago.

ESSAY 04

The Frankenstein effect
Toronto's built form

A two-decade building boom has reshaped Toronto, fusing old buildings with new. But are these mutated structures wonders or abominations?

by Alex Bozikovic, writer

A 42-storey skyscraper perched atop a Georgian villa? Bizarre as it may sound, that is the scene that greets you on Toronto's University Avenue, where a new residential tower by Zeidler Architects projects from the two-storey façade of the old Royal Canadian Military Institute. It's an awkward blend, serving neither the memory of the older building (essentially gone) nor the function of the present.

Such encounters are not uncommon in the downtown of this rapidly growing city; ambiguous preservation laws have birthed many such Frankensteins since the 1980s. Then, as now, high-rises shot up having been grafted onto bits of old houses or warehouses. A local critic complained of these "mutations": "When architects start playing around with genetics, monsters are inevitable."

Today, Toronto is nearly two decades into a building boom that has reshaped its core in radical ways, powered in part by sophisticated urbanists. This redevelopment

– with warehouse districts turning into vertical neighbourhoods, parks and squares – is big and bold.

Yet the city's culture has always been cautious and the Frankenstein tower, as a type, reflects this aspect of the civic spirit. Well into the 20th century, Toronto was small, colonial and devoutly Protestant. It was not a place for big plans. Now it has an ambivalent relationship to its past and most locals have little sense of the city's history. Even its more recent past, in which progressive urbanites (including writer and activist Jane Jacobs) rallied to save the fine grain of its older Victorian urbanism, remains somewhat obscure.

This is both a weakness and a strength. A weakness since the apparent lack of history makes it hard to define a civic identity: what is Toronto about, anyway? And a strength too, because that question remains open. To a remarkable degree, the city's very character is still being defined.

Downtown Toronto, the site of the smaller Victorian city, is ever popular; its population has doubled in recent times and may double again in another 25 years. This raises hard questions for heritage: which buildings should be kept, to retain aspects of the city's built form? The Frankenstein model is a poor one but many newer designs – thanks to forceful advocacy from local planners – aim to retain larger portions of older buildings, letting the past speak more clearly.

"Can you add housing and workplaces for thousands without gutting the past?"

And there are ways to meaningfully balance new developments with retention. Incrementalism has also been a positive part of the city's design culture. When they landed in 1960s Toronto, the architects Jack Diamond and Barton Myers brought a modernist language inspired by Louis Kahn as well as a respect for the existing fabric of the city. In projects such as the widely published York Square they added

Crisis talks
Community spirit

———

If something goes wrong in your life – be it a minor accident or a major, internationally significant event – you can rely on the people of Toronto to come to your aid.

*by Tomos Lewis,
Monocle*

Buildings that combine past and present

———

01 QRC West
This office block allows room for two loft buildings to remain.
02 The Royal Conservatory of Music
Victorian and modern.
03 Mars Discovery District
New research centre fronted by a 1912 façade.

---

new architecture behind and around the old. This sensitivity has been carried on by local firms such as KPMB, which elegantly bridged a high-Victorian pile with new modernist additions at the Royal Conservatory of Music.

The question is whether a conversation between the eras can be maintained when the present day has so much to say. Can you add housing and workplaces for hundreds of thousands of people without gutting the past? There is hope. For a building called QRC West, local architecture firm Sweeny & Co kept two ageing brick-and-beam industrial buildings – one as a rebuilt shell, one intact – and added a new sustainably designed 17-storey office tower above them. Resting on a clearly visible steel structure, it's a bravura piece of engineering that leaves the past in place while pointing to a denser, more interesting future. — (M)

ABOUT THE WRITER: Alex Bozikovic is the architecture critic for *The Globe and Mail*. He has also written for architecture and design publications including *Azure, Dwell, Architect* and *Wallpaper*. He is writing an architectural guide to Toronto, to be published in 2017.

It was just after five on a crisp March afternoon and I'd popped home from MONOCLE's Toronto bureau to pick something up. I closed my front door behind me, ready to head back to the office, walked down the steps of my porch and stepped onto the street.

Little did I know that there was a carpet of black ice on the pavement; the day's melting snow had frozen once more as the sun set. I stepped out, pirouetting across the pavement with the grace of an uncle at a wedding disco, and fell to the ground. Snap. My leg jammed beneath me and my ankle splintered in two.

Not only had I now completed my initiation into life in Canada, as my Canadian friends would tell me (winter injuries in Toronto, they said, are as predictable as the rising of the sun) but I was also about to experience one of this city's finest qualities: the unwavering ability to deal with a crisis. From tiny, personal dramas like my broken ankle, to larger, communal crises that impact neighbours and strangers alike, Toronto has a knack for coming up with the goods when times get tough.

For the next six weeks, as I hobbled around on crutches feeling sorry for myself, both friends and strangers rallied around. Groceries were bought, casseroles made, laundry done for me. Strangers would stop on the street and apologise for what had obviously befallen me. At watering holes across the city, drinks were bought for me.

On one occasion, while I was stranded on my crutches waiting for a streetcar, a woman in a big colourful knitted sweater, singing to herself as she walked along the street, asked if she could hail a cab for me. "My wolf whistle is famous in Toronto," she said. And, true to her word, spotting the little glowing taxi light three or four blocks away, she demonstrated her proficiency. The cab swerved to the edge of the pavement, stopped, and I was on my way. (Before our goodbyes she told me her name – Kathleen – and that she had once served as a school crosswalk warden. "They called me the singing crosswalk lady." The police suspended her, she told me, after she appeared in the music video of a local indie band, displaying her trademark dance moves. The crosswalks of Toronto are surely poorer places without her.)

"Toronto has a knack for coming up with the goods when times get tough"

But small acts of kindness are amplified here. And, when larger challenges raise their heads, it's the spirit of the singing crosswalk wardens, the cake-bakers and the general doers-of-good that comes to the fore.

When, in December, 2015, Canada's prime minister Justin Trudeau welcomed the first of an influx of refugees fleeing the Syrian civil war to Toronto's Pearson International Airport, people across the city – and indeed the whole country – swung into action to welcome those escaping the crisis. And, when it emerged that some Syrian children in Toronto weren't able

Three city heroes
───

01 Lester B Pearson
Regarded as the father of modern peacekeeping.
02 John Andrews
The architect behind the CN Tower.
03 Michelle DuBarry
At 85, one of the world's oldest performing drag queens.

to enroll in school without permanent addresses in the city (a process that can take a frustratingly long time), a group of teachers set up temporary classrooms for them so that their schooldays, halted by the war at home, wouldn't have to wait.

A similar spirit was displayed when a wildfire tore through the city of Fort McMurray in Alberta in early 2016: many Syrians who'd been offered a home in Canada donated the clothes that had been given to them when they arrived in the country to those whose lives had been turned to ashes by the fires.

Promoting a political solution to a crisis is one thing but when a spontaneous, public response swells behind it – or, quite frequently in Canada, independently of it – that, in my view, gives you a sense of the spirit of a place.

It would be rather rose-tinted of me to say that life in Toronto – and Canada more broadly – is an unfettered idyll. There are challenges here, of course: economic and social; rural and urban; domestic and imported. But, if you find yourself in a crisis, there are worse places to be than here. — (M)

ABOUT THE WRITER: Tomos Lewis is MONOCLE's bureau chief in Toronto. He previously worked as a producer for Monocle 24 radio and for BBC News in Washington. His ankle, thanks to Canada's excellent health service, is now fully healed.

ESSAY 06
Get your skates on
The home of hockey
———
Canada's national sport may well be lacrosse but there's no denying that ice hockey rules in the minds of its people. And in Toronto it's practically a religion.

by Dani Couture, writer

Welcome to Toronto: Hockey Capital of the World. Or so it likes to bill itself, given the fervour of the city's fans and the abundance of star players it produces. But when it comes to actual on-ice success, that claim is up for debate.

While lacrosse, invented by Canada's indigenous people, remains the country's official sport, it's hockey that ranks first in most people's hearts. As the Hockey Hall of Fame goes to great lengths to show, it's Canada where the sport was born and is still played most avidly, whatever the environs, from backyard rinks and frozen ponds to packed arenas. Though 23 of the 30 teams in the National Hockey League (NHL) are in the US, half the league's players are Canadian.

Unfortunately the only way most Torontonians – including players on the local pro team, the Maple Leafs – get to see or touch the sport's highest prize is by visiting the Hockey Hall of Fame located at the southern end of Yonge Street.

There, solemnly perched inside a vault that once belonged to the Bank of Montréal, resides the Stanley Cup, the 123-year-old trophy awarded to the team that wins the NHL's annual championship.

The vault is both fitting and something of a sour reminder to local fans, for the Montréal Canadiens – the Leafs' oldest and most-hated rivals – have won 24 cups to Toronto's 13. Worse still: Toronto hasn't won it since 1967, the longest drought of any team in the league. While hometown stars such as Drake, The Weeknd and even our pro baseball team, the Toronto Blue Jays, all seem to have captured the spotlight lately, the Leafs find themselves falling short time and again.

All the same, from October to May, hockey becomes a way of life in Toronto, more akin to religion than sport. The game is such a fixture in local mythology that it shows up almost everywhere, from public art (the "Hockey Knights in Canada" mural in College subway station) to indie rock tunes (Tragically Hip's "Fifty Mission Cap", which chronicles the disappearance of Leafs player Bill Barilko months after he scored the Cup-winning goal over the Canadiens in 1951).

"From October to May, hockey becomes a way of life in Toronto, more akin to religion than sport"

If the Leafs are in town, playing at the 20,000 seat Air Canada Centre, you shouldn't miss the opportunity to watch first-hand this most high-tempo of sports, equal parts ferocity and grace. The sound is like poetry to Canadian ears: the players' skates cutting into the ice as they fly after the puck; the puck slapping on stick blades. Feel the swelling of the crowd as a player brutally checks an opponent into the boards before performing an exquisite deke – a deceptive feint enabling the puck carrier to wheel round a defender – and going on to score the deciding goal.

Three hockey stars

01 Wayne Gretzky
Canada's most treasured sporting son.
02 Angela James
One of the first female professional hockey players.
03 Ken Dryden
Goalkeeper for the Montréal Canadiens.

Leafs fans are famous for always filling the seats and making noise, even if it includes occasional heckling of the home team. Arrive early and you can grab a cold beer and watch the players warm up at ice level. You might even catch a glimpse of beloved former Leafs captain Wendel Clark, who's rumoured to attend most home games. Clark remains a fan-favourite because of his grit and ability to rally the team while at the Leafs' helm. Small for a pro hockey player (5'11"), he was one of the toughest players in the league. Oh, and he could score too.

As any new Leafs player discovers, the level of media scrutiny here is like nowhere else. Even in summer, radio channels dissect every off-season move made by team management, or recall moments from the franchise's better days. And now, for the first time in years, there's a new optimism to the talk. Leafs fans are feeling something like hope thanks to the emergence of some genuinely talented prospects, the first such crop in a generation. It has some fans daring to think the unthinkable, that the team could pull off what it's only done once in the past decade: qualify for the Stanley Cup playoffs and perhaps be recognised as the world's hockey capital after all. — (M)

ABOUT THE WRITER: Born in Toronto, Dani Couture is a poet, novelist and a Wendel Clark fan. She still clings to the belief that the Toronto Maple Leafs will win the Stanley Cup in her lifetime, despite what her Québec-born Canadiens-loving father says.

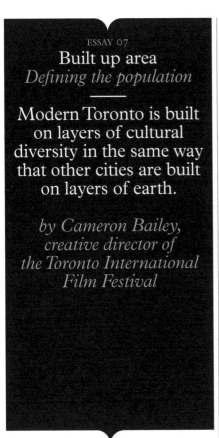

ESSAY 07
Built up area
Defining the population

Modern Toronto is built on layers of cultural diversity in the same way that other cities are built on layers of earth.

by Cameron Bailey, creative director of the Toronto International Film Festival

Toronto is a city of layers: beneath some streets, rivers still run; walk down certain pavements and you will see unfortunate houses all tilted in a row, where the waters have pushed the earth to one side. But it's more than just physical; this is a city where the people itself form distinct strata. Toronto's greatest layers are of demographic change.

Today, half of Toronto's citizens were born outside Canada, identifying as "visible minorities" – making nonsense of the word "minority" and turning Toronto into the most multicultural city on the planet.

But beneath the recent blanket of migrants from Asia, Latin America, Africa, the Caribbean and the Arab world sit earlier 20th-century seams. Coming from Europe, these people fled war and economic uncertainty for better lives in what they hoped was a more stable nation. Beneath that there are more layers still: the Irish, Scots and English who landed in Toronto aiming to build a new society. And further down again are those that founded Toronto, those who've lived the longest on this land and who may still tilt the city to their path: the indigenous people.

People have lived in what we now call Toronto for some 10,000 years. Were you to dig down past today's glass towers and asphalt, you could still find buried evidence of the Huron, Haudenosaunee, and Mississauga peoples from millennia ago. Once, the downtown intersection of King and John

Three indigenous Canadian peoples

---

01 Mississaugas
Lived on the Credit River at time of first European settlement.
02 Huron-Wendat
Lived on Lake Ontario's north shore until about 1650.
03 Haudenosaunee
A confederacy of five Iroquois nations.

streets – where cultural centre Tiff Bell Lightbox now sits – lay beneath the waters of Lake Iroquois; the shore, where hunters stalked giant mastodons, was farther north. The indigenous people, as local writer Suzanne Methot notes, used both the land and the rivers to build communities and sustain trade routes that ran all the way to the Gulf of Mexico.

"Toronto" itself is an Iroquois word that means "the place where trees stand in the water". And that's a perfect image for the city. Water both shaped and fed those trees, just as our history both shapes and feeds today's constantly shifting metropolis.

It's these layers of people and history that produce Toronto's unique cultural mix. But more than that, there's an openness to intermingling, whether that openness is conscious or not. There was a time when Toronto seemed frozen in sanctimony; legendary author and literary critic Northrop Frye once called it "a good place to mind your own business". As it turns out, that was a temporary season.

Way back in its past, Toronto was marked by movement of various indigenous groups and the agricultural need to move whole villages every 20 years or so, to allow the land to replenish itself. With new people crashing onto its shores for most of its history, the nature of the city itself meant that minding your own business was never going to be sustainable. As new people brought new customs, new languages, new food and new ideas, one had to adapt simply to navigate the city.

Today you can see the constant ebb and flow of Toronto's people at Pearson Airport but also in the thriving south-Asian communities that now surround it. You can see the city's new cultural confidence in Drake but also the black hip-hop clubs that gave birth to him. You can see the pride of the city every September during the Toronto International Film Festival. But if you want to see what feeds the festivals, look to Tiff's 3,000 volunteers and their dozens of different languages. Look to the unforced enthusiasm for difference found in Toronto's Caribbean carnival and Pride parades. Look to what we learned from 10,000 years of intermingling in the place where trees stand in the water. — (M)

"There's an openness to intermingling, whether it is conscious or not"

ABOUT THE WRITER: Cameron Bailey is Creative Director of the Toronto International Film Festival. He is also a board member of Tourism Toronto and teaches at the University of Toronto.

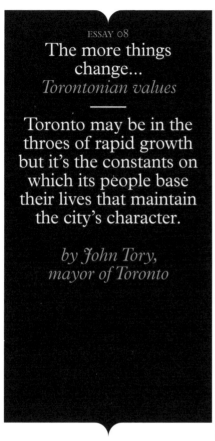

ESSAY 08
The more things change...
Torontonian values

Toronto may be in the throes of rapid growth but it's the constants on which its people base their lives that maintain the city's character.

by John Tory, mayor of Toronto

When I started my own family, my wife Barbara and I took our kids to Riverdale Farm. Today we go there with our grandchildren. The farm has changed over the years, along with the neighbouring areas (and I'm giving my age away when I say that I remember the zoo that originally occupied the site). But for all the developments of the passing decades, the pleasure I take from this rural oasis, where a sense of calm is underpinned by the muted hum of the surrounding city, is the same as when I first came here.

Toronto is a city that is rapidly transforming. But, like the sense of tranquillity offered at Riverdale Farm, there are things about it that remain unchanged: its beautiful public spaces, the quick ferry ride to Toronto Island Park and the city's famous ravines. These lush spaces give residents the opportunity to reflect, relax and create memories. Toronto's most well-known buildings have also been a reassuring constant: the CN Tower, the Rogers Centre and the Art Gallery of Ontario to name just a few.

But alongside these physical landmarks there is something immutable about the spirit of this city too: its sense of diversity. When you walk our streets and visit our neighbourhoods, which I do every day, I'm struck – as I always have been – by the variety of faces I see: all ages and colours, and a symphony of languages singing a similar tune as they go about their daily lives. That vibrant mix is enshrined in our motto: "Diversity our strength".

Every day I have the chance to hear the incredible stories of our residents, many of whom had to sacrifice a great deal to arrive in the city they now call home. They have struggled to obtain the basic freedoms that we so often take for granted in Canada but they do not turn their back on where they came from. I believe that we are all better for this healthy spirit of cultural differences.

One of my proudest moments as mayor was when a new community-revitalisation project was established in Lawrence Heights, where new Canadians from all over the world have settled after facing great hardships. Many of its residents have already been through too much and worked too hard, and they deserve their housing to provide the dignity and protection that they have earned. When the ageing townhouses finally began to be demolished to be replaced with something new, it was met with cheers from the community, who lean on each other for support during difficult times.

"We have beautiful spaces in which to play with our kids and we will have pockets of community where people hold each other up"

We are determined that this core value will continue to be unaffected by the necessary changes that Toronto will undergo.

We have beautiful spaces in which to play with our kids and pockets of community where people hold each other up. We are a city whose mayor marches in the Pride parade and who joins its citizens in welcoming Syrian refugees with open arms and open hearts.

Toronto's "constant" is not that its people are different: it is that we are able to come together and celebrate these differences, in our quiet places and with our fierce sense of pride. — (M)

Three immigrant groups
—
01 South Asian
The largest ethnic group in Toronto.
02 Caribbean
One of the largest Caribbean communities in North America.
03 Italian
Italians first arrived in Toronto in the 1870s.

ABOUT THE WRITER: John Tory was elected mayor of Toronto in October 2014. He started as a radio journalist before a career in law; then, as a political strategist, he managed the campaigns of former Canadian prime ministers Brian Mulroney and Kim Campbell.

Wander woman
Jane's Walk

Based on the writings of activist Jane Jacobs, a programme now exists that encourages people to walk for the sake of walking. And it could be the best way to get to know Toronto's neighbourhoods.

by Denise Pinto, landscape architect

Here's a thing I find baffling when travelling to a new city: most travel guides tend only to emphasise geography. Climb this mountain, they say; visit this attraction.

It's an efficient way to categorise a city's parts, I suppose: to define its functions and locales – its limbs – and map them out in neat, pre-certified points of interest. "Here's our tallest tower and over here, a big and popular public park." You might think that as a landscape architect who loves a good map I would have an allegiance to this approach – but I don't. It just shows the well traversed, well rehearsed and well endorsed.

But there is so much more to our cities than this. How can you begin to know a place if you only learn its geography and perhaps the small fragment of its history that is written? So much more is unwritten. So much more is being created every day. And the people who live in a city – the locals – are the ones who hold the key.

So let's take our lead from Jane Jacobs, a woman whose memory is at the heart of an international walking project that I've been at the helm of for some years now: Jane's Walk.

The project gets people to host walking tours for their neighbours, showing off the everyday, the ordinary and the extraordinary about the places they frequent. That might mean an unassuming building where a resident will cook you Tibetan *momos* (dumplings) and tell you jokes (Loga's Corner in Parkdale, for those wondering) or a collective of local women, mostly immigrants from south Asia, who worked with the City to put a tandoor oven in a park so that they could live-fire bread (Thorncliffe Park, if you're playing along). I picked two food examples because I think that's what'll get your attention, dear reader, but the list goes on. The places may be mappable but their significance and sweetness are in the connection to our collective humanity.

Jane exemplified this. In case you don't know, she was an author and activist who wrote a number of influential pieces about what she saw in the transforming neighbourhoods around her: tight-knit communities being dismantled to make way for progress, freeways and cars. A prudent observer of cities, she looked compassionately at the streets and pavements around her and saw them not only for their bricks-and-mortar existence but also their social value. And she did this by walking. A lot.

This is something we can all take to heart. Part of learning about any city is not only knowing its places but also its people. To do that, we walk. We go slowly, we make time, we amble and we wander.

One time I followed a cat. Down the street and around the corner to a parkette

at the end of the road. The route was full
of little surprises: a crepe-paper banner
along a fence; the half-washed pavement
where hopscotch markings peeked
through fallen leaves; a brilliantly
plumed cardinal in a nearby tree. The
cat eventually paused at a hedgerow and
darted under it, ending my serendipitous
jaunt in front of a tiny boy selling
lemonade. I got into a discussion with
his watchful sister about a park down the
street. "There's buried treasure there," she
told me matter-of-factly. So I went. It was
a great and unexpected way to see
something new and to be pulled off the
beaten path. It was a neighbourhood I
didn't know well but she was an expert;
she lived there, after all.

It made me wonder: when visiting
a neighbourhood apart from your own,
how can you tell what novel uses of public
space abound? So much gets overlooked
in the yawning monotony of daily routine.
The toughest tourists are always the locals
themselves. Getting outside your bubble
requires a dedicated approach to
wandering and
discovery that is
equally laden with
social value: the
suggestions of
strangers. Seeing
the city through
the eyes of a local,
as it turns out, is a
way to see not just the places that are
spelled out on a map but also the people
and the ideas that rouse them. It's nice to
be taken by the hand and shown the way.

*"Travelling,
truly travelling,
is seeing not
just the city
but seeing
each other"*

That grove of trees you pass on your
commute? Well, that might just have been
planted by a deaf environmental activist
on Earth Day since 1981 (Johann Fisch, to
be specific, and the orchard is beside the
Applewood Shaver House in Etobicoke).
Or maybe the community centre you've
walked by for years actually fills its
swimming pool with rainbow trout so that
inner-city kids can learn to fish (Scadding
Court Community Centre). Or perhaps

> **Three Jane
> Jacobs milestones**
> —
> **01** Architectural Forum (1952)
> Campaigning to modernise
> established urban areas.
> **02** The Death and Life of
> Great American Cities (1961)
> Her first, most famous book.
> **03** Dark Age Ahead (2004)
> Her last book warned of
> cultural decay.

you've never been to the Cedarbrae
library, which, when the sun sinks in
the sky on any given Wednesday, is filled
with young people printing 3D toys
they whipped up on publicly accessible
modelling software.

We encourage people to walk for
walking's sake, to look closely at what's
around them and discover – or rediscover
– the phenomena of the everyday. During
our big global festival on the first week of
May each year, the whole world walks
together. Over 1,000 tours in nearly 25
languages across six continents practise
the art of public wandering.

On one night walk with therapist Oona
Fraser, the silent crowd listened to poetry by
the light of a single lit sparkler. Some of the
most spectacular visions of Swansea were
seen that evening: wetlands that looked
otherworldly, glinting in the dark; the tree
canopy above, backlit by street lamps;
people's bodies in the silence, cracking twigs
underfoot, rustling against fences and
looking out for each other. Fraser organises
regular walks; the pace is fast and the
climbs are challenging but it's worth it for
the confrontation with darkness and the
enduring smell of magnolias.

At Jane's Walk we talk about how
walking the city is a gateway to "urban
literacy". A terse, inscrutable term, it's
true. But it means three very simple
things: knowing what's around you (travel
guides, you do well in this department);
knowing who's around you (your
neighbours, the butcher, baker or yes,

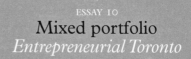

even the candlestick maker); and knowing your own place in this system, your relationship to what's around you. It's a distilled version of the aptitudes that Jane Jacobs brought together in her writing. Now, having passed Jacobs' 100th year, I think the timing is right to pay a little more attention, to dig deep and to get "literate" about the city.

Travelling, truly travelling, is seeing not just the city but seeing each other. It's about developing bonds and connecting, even if ephemerally. So hit the streets and discover the phenomena of the everyday. At the very least, your stories of our city will offer an alternative to the CN Tower that will delight a total stranger. — (M)

ABOUT THE WRITER: Denise Pinto is a landscape architect and executive director of the Jane's Walk project. In 2016, she was named a Vital Person by the Toronto Foundation in recognition of the work she has done to make a difference in the city. Jane's Walk tours are posted online at *janeswalk.org*; all of them are free, with no registration needed.

ESSAY 10

Mixed portfolio
Entrepreneurial Toronto

___

The city's blend of cultures and ethnicities is responsible for some of its most creative start-ups and businesses.

by Tim Draimin, social innovator

London's mayor, Sadiq Khan, recently stated that the British capital is the most diverse city in the world. Some of us would gently refute that claim: with 200-plus nationalities converging in Toronto, the stats put this city by the lake out front for the title. Whether that's fair or not, Toronto always shows up near the top of any list of the world's most multicultural cities. It's a badge of honour.

And it is our strength. The cross-cultural combination and convergence of creativity, experiences, aspirations, passions and ambitions bubble together, sparking an avid entrepreneurialism and grit. It produces everything and everyone from Pablum to Lorne Michaels (who creates *Saturday Night Live*), as well as to the Raptors (that's the grit), Kobo Books, Imax, Nanoleaf and dozens of start-ups on the cusp of radically innovating our daily lives in one way or another.

Our border-crossing citizenry reinforces a border-spanning zeitgeist.

Torontonians have a legacy for blasting through assumptions and stereotypes, unlocking the untapped potential of individuals and communities and developing or capturing new, unimagined markets to boot.

Our diversity means that there's a market for almost anything; not only are you likely to find a sustainable fan base that wants to spend evenings axe-throwing or pairing cocktails and offal but also a thriving audience for social entrepreneurs to reimagine how we eat (Tiffinday's pulse-based curries), invest (Purpose Capital's impact-investing advisory), buy energy (Bullfrog Power's green energy retail) and more.

It also means that we are connected to communities and markets in almost every country around the world. We share our stories, ideas and successes with our families and cultures abroad, as well as both importing and exporting our best innovations and businesses.

But what brings all these people together? What is Toronto's magnetism? It may have something to do with being a globally competitive marketplace, home to the Toronto Stock Exchange, as well as major global headquarters such as Four Seasons Hotels and Resorts and Brookfield Asset Management. We've attracted the Canadian offices of Facebook, Airbnb, Autodesk and Apple into Downtown, as well as the first Johnson & Johnson Innovation – Jlabs incubator – outside the US.

"It's not hard to look at the global rankings that list us at the top of liveability, trendiness and entrepreneurship and link it back to a city that is open to hearts, minds and voices"

It may have something to do with the concentration of catalytic universities here. That includes the University of Toronto, a public-research collegiate university that is nearly 200 years old; York University, home to Canada's only space-engineering programme, OCAD University, an experimental arts-and-design hub; and Ryerson University, a career-focused institution and Ashoka U designated campus, which prioritises lived experience and encourages student entrepreneurs through programmes such as the DMZ, the top-ranked university-based incubator in North America. Add half a dozen technology colleges and there is a kaleidoscope of ambitious young talent in Toronto.

But we are more than the sum of our parts; there is a real purpose behind Toronto's support for business creativity. Leading the way is one of the world's largest urban innovation sectors: the Mars Discovery District. Born as a medical commercialisation hub for the network of research undertaken at Toronto's universities and hospitals, Mars is an example of what attracts start-ups and giants alike to this city.

If all the world's a stage, Torontonians try to set that stage for entrepreneurialism to thrive. And we aren't boxed in by the walls of the arena. The city blends into the greater Toronto area and, specifically, into the Toronto–Kitchener–Waterloo corridor. It's a confluence of researchers, incubators, accelerators and investment anchored in the southwest by the University of Waterloo, BlackBerry, Communitech, Google's biggest R&D

Three Toronto inventions

01 The lightbulb
Henry Woodward patented the lightbulb in Toronto in 1874.
02 Insulin
Developed by University of Toronto researchers in 1922.
03 The whoopee cushion
Created in 1930 by the JEM Rubber Company.

office in Canada and, in the near future, the world's largest Internet of Things manufacturing space, called Catalyst137.

What does all of this say about Toronto? That we seek to keep the door open to opportunities that will support innovation. But it also comes back to our social entrepreneurs. Toronto's entrepreneurship has a unique sense of community, where the development of new business is pursued as a means to a more sustainable, healthy or inclusive end. It was here that Dr John Mighton started a tutoring club and realised that the barrier holding children back from maths excellence was the belief that either you got it or you didn't. While tutoring students, Dr Mighton developed a numeracy programme on the premise that all children can be led to think mathematically, giving birth to the acclaimed Jump Math programme.

Toronto social innovator Tonya Surman similarly tapped into the unseen power of society with the invention of the Community Bond, a new financial mechanism for non-profit capital projects. With four spaces in operation in Toronto, the Centre for Social Innovation both exemplifies Toronto's drive and fuels it.

Our greatest driver is our desire to invest in our communities, our society and each other, against complex challenges that necessitate an inclusive creativity that the world's most diverse city can provide. With so many different cultures living together we must continue to make Toronto even more equitable. We are not nirvana. But it's not hard to look at the global rankings that list us at the top of liveability, trendiness and entrepreneurship and link it back to a city that is open to hearts, minds and voices and most importantly, perhaps, open for business too. — (M)

ESSAY 11

Sing when you're winning
The Four Seasons Centre

In order to announce itself as a truly global destination, a city needs an acoustically magnificent opera house. And now Toronto has just that.

by Sarah Fulford, writer and editor

For the past few decades of the 20th century, many people in Toronto bemoaned the fact that the city had no opera house. Back then the Canadian Opera Company (COC) performed in a drab multipurpose event space (now called The Sony Centre) which had notoriously bad acoustics. To be a truly great global city – like New York, Buenos Aires or Sydney – Toronto needed a big, bold, beautiful platform for its opera and ballet. For a while a great many hopes and dreams hung on the promise of an opera house.

Then, in 2006, after years of lobbying and fundraising, Toronto got its wish: a 2,000-plus capacity auditorium dedicated to opera and ballet called The Four Seasons

ABOUT THE WRITER: Tim Draimin, Toronto-born global citizen, is executive director of Social Innovation Generation, an ecosystem catalyst operating from both Mars Discovery District and Centre for Social Innovation.

Centre (the Toronto-based owner of the Four Seasons hotel chain donated $20 million to the project).

The design of the building initially ruffled a few feathers: the exterior is stark, like a giant black box that has descended from space. But at night the whole thing comes magically alive.

The building is at the corner of University Avenue and Queen Street, in the heart of the city. It's close to city hall, the Ontario courthouses, several big banks and the restaurants where the city's most powerful people meet. Massive glass windows in its west-facing wall turn the bustle of the city into a mesmerising spectacle for operagoers to enjoy. I love a drink in the lobby during intermission, looking down at the hustle and bustle below.

But the greatest triumph is the horseshoe-shaped hall itself. It is both casual and sophisticated at the same time, and it has magnificent acoustics. Johannes Debus, the opera company's German-born music director, came to Toronto as guest conductor in 2009 and stayed permanently, in part because the sound quality in the hall is so good. Sondra Radvanovsky, one of the world's best sopranos, lives just outside Toronto but didn't start making regular appearances with the COC until the Four Seasons Centre was built.

Three years after the opening, Toronto scored a second first-rate space for music performance: Koerner Hall. Affiliated with the Royal Conservatory at Bloor and St George, the hall is connected elegantly to the conservatory's red-brick building from the 1880s. Koerner Hall is my favourite place to enjoy music because the space is intimate yet grand. Once, my husband and I heard the Latvian-born Israeli cellist Mischa Maisky

"Both casual and sophisticated, the hall has magnificent acoustics"

perform three of the Bach unaccompanied suites there. It was the second half of his full day's recital of all six suites – a major mental and physical challenge. Maisky, who is in his seventies, was sweating so much that he changed his colourful billowing cotton shirt between each suite. Koerner Hall was built for such one-man performances: every brush of his bow could be heard throughout the room.

I grew up in Toronto and studied cello well into my university days. As a teenager there was nowhere great to hear classical music. For a few years I had a subscription to a terrific quartet series in a depressing hall with all the charm of a high-school auditorium. To this day the Toronto Symphony plays in a building that is stuck in the 1980s – all lush grey lobby carpets and brass banisters – with acoustics so soupy I never feel like going. So imagine my surprise and joy that

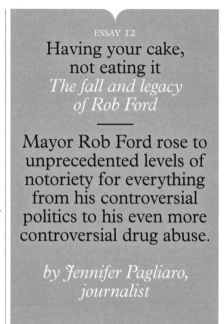
**Three unusual
Toronto music venues**

01 Toronto Music Garden
Outdoor lakeshore venue.
02 Integral House
Private residence on the ravine
built to host concerts.
03 Trinity St Pauls Centre
Renovated church that is home
to Baroque ensemble
Tafelmusik.

two great halls were built in Toronto
in my lifetime.

Said halls were built in a time of
incredible growth in the city, when
population numbers surpassed
those of Chicago's. With all the
new people came a new set of
expectations, ambitions, money
and global tastes. Fortunately the
new Toronto now has the music
venues to match. — (M)

ABOUT THE WRITER: Sarah Fulford was born in
Toronto and is the editor in chief of *Toronto Life*
magazine. She has lived in New York and Jerusalem.
She spent much of her adolescence practising
Bach's cello suites.

ESSAY 12

Having your cake, not eating it
The fall and legacy of Rob Ford

Mayor Rob Ford rose to
unprecedented levels of
notoriety for everything
from his controversial
politics to his even more
controversial drug abuse.

*by Jennifer Pagliaro,
journalist*

It was my third day on the city hall beat
for the *Toronto Star*, our city's best-read
newspaper. I had spent a quiet morning
interviewing a longshot candidate in the
upcoming municipal election before trying
to get my bearings inside what we
affectionately call the "Clamshell", so
named for the domed council chamber
nestled between two towers in Downtown.

That April evening I returned home
to find my roommate ordering a takeaway.
She added a slice of chocolate cake onto
her order for me. Just after the delivery
arrived I got an email: Rob Ford, then
mayor of Toronto, was taking a leave
of absence after a year of scandal over
substance abuse.

The shock was palpable. Rushing to the
office I abandoned the cake on the coffee
table and, figuring that pyjamas weren't
appropriate attire for the newsroom, left
my room strewn with clothes.

This was the unpredictable madness of
the Ford days, for which I briefly and

unforgettably had a front-row seat. Much of that early view was of the path between our press gallery, crammed into city hall's rear wings, and the glass-walled reception area of the mayor's office that became known as the "fish bowl".

During the second half of Ford's term the doors were often locked and guarded by security. By that point reporters had to shout questions as the mayor passed swiftly to and from a lift to the parking garage, prevented from getting too close to the man at the centre of the biggest story in town.

The election campaign that followed took me to the outer edges of the city, exposing divides unseen even by most locals: a mother begging for locks that would actually work on the doors of her decrepit social housing, at the same time as senior citizens seeking a comfortable retirement insisted that taxes to pay for repairs to crumbling infrastructure were already too high. Commuters crammed onto a crowded transit system that badly needed relief, while suburban motorists continued to insist that the "war on cars" was alive and well.

"This was the unpredictable madness of the Ford days, for which I briefly and unforgettably had a front-row seat"

This was Toronto under Ford, and the space between the end of his mayoralty and the campaign of his successor John Tory was an education in the story of Toronto as a city of divides.

At the tail end of the 2014 campaign I followed Tory on a weekend marathon to tour all 44 of the city's wards in 72 hours – an exhausting stunt to highlight his message of "One Toronto", a united city. This was after Ford's crack scandal and after he was withdrawn from mayoral re-election, deemed too sick to go on. (He died in March 2016 after undergoing treatment for a rare form of cancer.)

However, despite Tory's triumphant election victory and Toronto's collective exhalation, traces of Ford's divisive politics and contradictions still linger at city hall, where an unwillingness to spend taxpayers' money has left critical programmes unfunded.

But the depth of those divides were still little known to me late on that April night when I returned to my apartment in Chinatown. I opened the fridge to find my cake safely tucked away in its takeout container. My second roommate had come home to find my mess and had done her best to piece together what had happened. She assumed correctly that when I got home, I'd still need the cake.

In the year that followed there would be other cakes: a sad birthday slice at Ford's campaign office, one he would never eat because he was in rehab. Then, months later, there would be cake for soon-to-be mayor John Tory – the big-slab kind, with an inexplicable essay scrawled in icing by a local bakery endorsing his campaign efforts.

Right then though, I grabbed a clean fork and dug back in to my own slice, ready – or not – for day four at city hall. — (M)

ABOUT THE WRITER: Jennifer Pagliaro is a city-hall reporter for the *Toronto Star* newspaper. In 2013 she was awarded the Goff Penny award for outstanding young journalists working in newspapers.

Culture
—— Broaden your mind

Over the past few years Toronto has added to its rich cultural pedigree with a burgeoning reputation as a festival city. A slew of newer music events throughout the summer – from Field Trip to the UK's Bestival franchise – have all pitched up in vibrant fashion. They complement Toronto's homegrown offerings, such as the world-renowned Toronto International Film Festival and well-regarded 10-day Toronto Jazz Festival.

There are more offbeat gems to enjoy here too, including a plethora of fabled music bars (where bands such as the Rolling Stones cut their teeth) and open-mic rap, poetry and spoken word events, performances by theatre and comedy companies and a fine selection of contemporary art galleries. You won't have to search too hard to see why Toronto's cultural offering is one of the city's most colourful assets.

Public exhibtion venues
The art beat

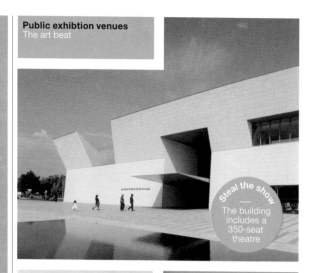

Steal the show
—
The building includes a 350-seat theatre

①
Aga Khan Museum,
Flemingdon Park
Shedding light

When the Aga Khan wrote to Japanese architect Fumihiko Maki asking him to design a museum around the concept of light, Maki responded in striking style. Built 45-degrees to true north so that daylight can stream into the galleries, the museum's walls are of luminous white Brazilian granite, set around a traditional four-part garden with reflective pools to mirror the sky.

The museum is dedicated to the arts of the Islamic world with a permanent collection of 1,000 objects spanning more than 10 centuries.
77 Wynford Drive, M3C 1K1
+1 416 646 4677
agakhanmuseum.org

Thursday-night gallery crawl

Art galleries and exhibition spaces in Toronto typically open new shows on Thursday evenings, so it's a good night to get a street-level feel for the city's rambunctious art scene. To find out what's on, check out *Now* online.
nowtoronto.com

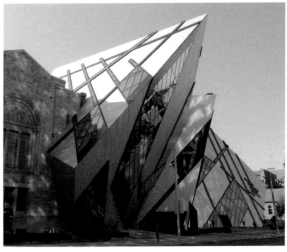

 The Gardiner Museum, Discovery
District
Celebrated ceramics

Canada's only gallery dedicated
to ceramics was opened in 1984
by George and Helen Gardiner to
showcase their private collection
of pottery. It spans the ancient
Americas, ceramics from 17th
and 18th-century Europe, Japan
and China, majolica-ware from
renaissance Italy and contemporary
pieces. In addition to cultural events,
the Gardiner also has a pottery
studio for pre-booked and drop-in
lessons. The limestone façade
designed by Toronto's KPMB was
added in 2006.
111 Queens Park, M5S 2C7
+1 416 586 8080
gardinermuseum.on.ca

Royal Ontario Museum,
Discovery District
Comprehensive collection

The Royal Ontario Museum was
founded in 1914 and is home to
more than six million objects. A
daring new wing designed by Daniel
Libeskind was added in 2007; The
Crystal, as it has become known,
was inspired by the mineralogy
collection. The Museum Station
subway stop features columns that
reflect the exhibits above ground
and were created by Diamond
Schmidtt Architects in 2008.
    The collection is complemented
by a rich roster of events spanning
lectures, tours and workshops.
100 Queens Park, M5S 2C6
+1 416 586 8000
rom.on.ca

③
Bata Shoe Museum, Discovery
District
Sole searching

"We don't just tell the story of shoes:
we tell the story of people through
shoes," says Bata Shoe Museum's
director Emanuele Lepri. Dating
to the 1940s, the collection was
begun by Sonja Bata, wife of shoe
magnate Thomas J Bata. Among
its exploration of the history of
global footwear is an indigenous
shoe collection that details Canada's

past through the "ingenuity of the
First Nations and Inuit people".
The museum was designed by
Raymond Moriyama.
327 Bloor Street West, M5S 1W7
+1 416 979 7799
batashoemuseum.ca

⑤
The Power Plant, Harbourfront
Contemporary powerhouse

Opened in 1987, this is the
country's leading non-collecting
public contemporary-art gallery.
Well-regarded Canadian artists
including Stan Douglas, Janet
Cardiff and George Bures Miller
have exhibited here but new work
by emerging artists from around
the globe is a regular fixture too.
Admission is free and the displays
are housed in a former power
plant, which was built in 1926
and decommissioned in 1980. Its
annual Power Ball, one of Toronto's
biggest and most colourful arts
events, takes place each summer.
231 Queens Quay West, M5J 2G8
+1 416 973 4949
thepowerplant.org

⑥
Art Gallery of Ontario, Chinatown
National pride

The Art Gallery of Ontario (originally the Art Museum of Toronto) boasts one of the largest art collections in North America, although only a fraction of its 90,000 pieces are on show at a time. The extensive displays range from painting and photography to sculpture, not to mention Canada's largest archive of African art. As well as an excellent schedule of visiting shows, the great appeal is the Canadian collection; the biggest in the country, it includes fine paintings by the celebrated Group of Seven.

The gallery reopened in 2008 following an extensive renovation by US-Canadian architect Frank Gehry, whose curved wood and glass façade spans an entire city block. His swirling wooden central staircase inside the museum has become a landmark in its own right.
317 Dundas Street West, M5T 1G4
+1 416 979 6648
ago.net

Commercial galleries
Wall-to-wall exhibits

Junction Triangle in a warehouse-like space with stark walls and polished concrete floors. With four to six shows per year, the gallery stresses quality and impact over quantity.

"We want to further the dialogue on contemporary art in Canada," says Toronto director Gareth Brown-Jowett. "The role of education and community-building is an important element of our mandate."
45 Ernest Avenue, M6P 3M7
+1 647 346 9082
arsenalmontreal.com

②
Corkin Gallery, Distillery District
Photography focus

Jane Corkin started her photography collection in the 1970s when the form was beginning to find a place in art galleries. After meeting renowned Hungarian-American photographer André Kertész she organised her first exhibit and, in 1978, founded the Corkin Gallery (originally the Jane Corkin Gallery). Today the gallery is located in a previously abandoned tank house and has featured pieces by the likes of Harry Callahan, Nan Goldin and Robert Frank. The gallery also hosts artist talks, workshops and concerts.
7 Tank House Lane, M5A 3C4
+1 416 979 1980
corkingallery.com

Arsenal Toronto, Junction Triangle
Edgy and educational

Though its first and largest location is in Montréal, Arsenal has settled naturally into its second home in

③
Daniel Faria Gallery,
Junction Triangle
Unique approach

Housed in an airy former
industrial space in Junction
Triangle, Daniel Faria Gallery
showcases work by 10 acclaimed
international and Canadian
artists, including Douglas
Coupland, Kristine Moran
and Elizabeth Zvonar.
　"I look for artists with unique
voices, offering something new
and different," says owner Daniel
Faria. "I want to create a gallery
in Toronto that feels international."
The gallery stages six to eight
shows each year.
188 St Helens Avenue, M6H 4A1
+ 1 416 538 1880
danielfariagallery.com

④
Diaz Contemporary, Niagara Village
Canadian/Mexican melding

Diaz Contemporary director
Benjamin Diaz – who also founded
the Galeria Arte Contemporáneo
and the Fundacion Para el Arte
Contemporáneo in Mexico –
spent 20 years travelling between
Mexico and Canada before
deciding to open a space in
Toronto. Works on display are by
artists such as James Carl, Pierre
Dorion and Francisco Castro. The
gallery is also known for its canine
mascot Luna, who can be spotted
in the gallery some Saturdays.
100 Niagara Street, M5V 1C5
+ 1 416 361 2972
diazcontemporary.ca

①
Hot Docs Ted Rogers Cinema,
The Annex
Docs in the house

Documentary film has a dedicated
home in Toronto: the century-old
Hot Docs Ted Rogers Cinema.
Considered one of the leading
theatres dedicated to non-fiction
film in North America, it's also the
hub of the annual citywide Hot
Docs festival, the largest showcase
of documentary films in the world.
　The cinema manages a fine
schedule of first-run Canadian
non-fiction film alongside a well-
curated roster of international
examples of the form.
　The cinema is a central fixture
in the so-called Bloor Street
Culture Corridor in the heart of
The Annex neighbourhood, an
arts initiative that was launched
back in 2014. Its dark, terraced
auditorium was modernised in
2012 by Toronto's Hariri Pontarini
architecture firm.
506 Bloor Street West, M5S 1Y3
+ 1 416 637 3123
hotdocscinema.ca

Toronto on film

01 Nobody Waved Goodbye, 1964:
With Hollywood so close, Canadian film-makers were slow to start making fiction features, focusing instead on documentary. But this poignant drama about a disaffected Toronto teen, shot on location in the city, helped trigger a wave of English-language cinema.

02 Dead Ringers, 1988:
No one captures the unsettling undertow of the city as well as David Cronenberg and this chilling drama about twin doctors is his masterpiece.

03 The Adjuster, 1991:
Edgy erotic drama from acclaimed Canadian director Atom Egoyan that captures the city in atmospheric widescreen.

04 Scott Pilgrim vs the World, 2010:
This hip comedy set in the Toronto suburbs stars Ontario-born Michael Cera as a young musician pitched against the seven exes of his love interest.

05 Stories We Tell, 2012:
A dazzling blend of recreation and documentary about Toronto-born actor-director Sarah Polley's childhood.

②
Tiff Bell Lightbox, Entertainment District
Cultural powerhouse

With the opening of Tiff Bell Lightbox in 2010, the Toronto International Film Festival has been able to elevate the city's cultural profile year round. Its six cinemas, exhibitions and learning centres and shop stocked with film-studies books make it an edificatory supercentre in the Entertainment District. Designed by architecture firm KPMB, the building is itself a sort of cinema; the large upper windows catch the shadows of those inside and project them onto its surface.
350 King Street West, M5V 3X5
+1 416 599 8433
tiff.net

③
Fox Theatre, The Beaches
Much-loved epic

The Fox Theatre dates back to 1914 and is now the oldest continuously operating cinema in Canada. Screening a mix of independent and foreign films as well as cult classics and new releases, the single-screen theatre's 248-seat auditorium has continued to keep up with the times. It has been a symbol of the neighbourhood's inherent charms for many a year and a quiet totem to the city's long love affair with film. There is also a small, fully licensed bar, as well as the usual movie snacks.
2236 Queen Street East, M4E 1G2
+1 416 691 7335
foxtheatre.ca

④
The Royal, Little Italy
Theatre landmark

The Royal is one of Toronto's most cherished landmarks, thanks partly to its elongated art deco-style frontage. Threatened with closure in 2007, the 390-seater was bought by the innovative Theatre D Digital production company.

While The Royal screens a selection of art house and indie films in the evenings, it also serves as a post-production studio, providing facilities to Canadian directors from Deepa Mehta to Atom Egoyan. It also runs a Kung-Fu Fridays series and The Royal Mystery Movie Night.
608 College Street, M6G 1B4
+1 416 466 4400
theroyal.to

Laugh it up
—
The venue also offers comedy classes

⑤
The Revue, Roncesvalles Village
Surviving the censors

When The Revue cinema opened in 1912 there was widespread suspicion of the moving image and Torontonians signed a petition seeking to close it. "Police would often come in with scissors and cut the rolls of movies they didn't like," says programming director Eric Veillette. But The Revue prevailed and remains one of the city's most evocative screening rooms.

Once it screened only German-language films; today it hosts everything from silent films to blockbusters, as well as panels with actors and film-makers.
400 Roncesvalles Avenue, M6R 2M9
+1 416 531 9950
revuecinema.ca

①
Comedy Bar, Christie Pits
Bar ha ha

Gary Rideout (*pictured, bottom*) used to spend his Sunday nights performing new shows across the city with his comedy troupe The Sketchersons. "I always thought there was room in the city for a space where comedy could be at the front and centre," he says.

After four years of venue-hopping, Rideout and his business partner James Elksnitis made the decision to launch Comedy Bar in 2008. Established as a place for emerging performers to showcase their talents, it has flourished. "It is rare to find a venue where you can choose between a different sketch, improv or stand-up all in the same night; there really is a genuine community feel to it across all genres of comedy," says Rideout.
945 Bloor Street West, M6H 1L5
+1 416 551 6540
comedybar.ca

Alright goosie, step on it – we're late for the film

Homegrown record labels

Indie record labels may be the backbone of Toronto's thriving, eclectic music scene but they've also helped to provide a platform for wider North American success.

01 Arts & Crafts Records:
Canada's premier indie label, A&C is best known as the home of Feist, Broken Social Scene and BadBadNotGood.
arts-crafts.ca

02 Paper Bag Records:
Paper Bag is a standard bearer for Canada's cutting-edge artists, from the experimental sounds of Tim Hecker and the cool techno-minimalism of Austra to kabuki-inspired prog-punkers Yamantaka// Sonic Titan.
paperbagrecords.com

03 Last Gang Records:
Its catalogue offers a little bit of everything but it really excels with indie rock, dance and electronica.
lastgang.com

(2)

National Ballet of Canada, Entertainment District
Tutu good

The National Ballet of Canada was founded in 1951 and now resides at The Four Seasons Centre for the Performing Arts (the first theatre in Canada designed specifically for both ballet and opera). The venue's quietly grand auditorium has some of the country's best acoustics, ideal for the company's full-length classical and contemporary works. "Our repertoire is so diverse, I still feel challenged and inspired," says principal dancer Sonia Rodriguez, who has been with the National Ballet since 1990.
145 Queen Street West, M5H 4G1
+1 416 345 9595
national.ballet.ca

(3)

Soulpepper Theatre Company, Distillery District
Theatrical heavy hitters

This artist-founded theatre company is the largest employer of theatrical artists in Toronto. It was launched in 1998 and produces a wide range of work, including classics, contemporary adaptations, musicals and concerts, not to mention a programme of weekly cabarets and touring shows. It also seeks to forge links with the community through various outreach programmes.

Housed in the Young Centre for the Performing Arts, Soulpepper Theatre spans two converted red-brick tank houses in the Distillery District.

"The actors have the opportunity to dig deeper here," says Albert Schultz, Soulpepper's founding artistic director. "They present incredible work."
50 Tank House Lane, M5A 3C4
+1 416 866 8666
soulpepper.ca

(4)

Factory Theatre, King West Village
Canadian-crafted content

Factory's diverse programme showcases the work of Canadian playwrights. "We aim to bring the cultural diversity that we experience on the streets of Toronto onto the stage and to the audience," says artistic director Nina Lee Aquino.

The venue's two buildings are among the most romantic theatre venues in the city: a Queen Anne gothic revival house, built in 1869, and a 1910 extension. Many features of the building are original, including the proscenium arch and balcony in the main auditorium.
125 Bathurst Street, M5V 2R2
+1 416 504 9971
factorytheatre.ca

⑤
Canadian Opera Company,
Entertainment District
Access all arias

In most cities the opera house is a
symbol of the past, of aristocratic
exclusivity and grandeur. Not so in
Toronto. The glass-and-steel building
of the Four Seasons Centre for
the Performing Arts is a strikingly
modern home for this traditional
artform. "The result is an electric
exchange," says Alexander Neef,
the group's German-born director.
Attracting world-class talent, the
company puts opera at the centre
of Toronto's artistic life and has
garnered international attention
in the process.
145 Queen Street West, M5H 4G1
+ 1 416 345 6671
coc.ca

⑥
Poetry Jazz Café, Kensington
Market
Low-key and laidback

The intimate Poetry Jazz Café, in
the heart of Kensington Market,
was designed to be a homely,
contemporary twist on jazz bars of
old. "I never wanted Poetry to have
a multiple-personality problem,"
says owner Sean Pascalle. "We have
a clear vision and stick to it."
  Performances take place in an
alcove at the front, the walls of
which are lined with paintings of
jazz greats. Look for the mural of
Miles Davis by Mexican painter
Carlos Delgado or just follow the
sound of the music.
224 Augusta Avenue, M5T 2L7
+ 1 416 599 5299
poetryjazzcafe.com

①
Adelaide Hall, Entertainment
District
Small yet mighty

While many live-music venues
in the city boast intimate settings,
few live up to the experience
offered by the newly reincarnated
Adelaide Hall. The venue was
downsized and reopened in 2015,
allowing it to play to its strengths
as a small space – it is also
something of a hidden gem thanks
to its backstreet entrance. Despite
its compact size, Adelaide Hall
attracts a roster of large names and
personalities, most of whom will
leave your ears ringing well after
the end of the show.
250 Adelaide Street West M5H 1X6
+ 1 647 344 1234
adelaidehallto.com

②
Mod Club, Little Italy
Promising noises

Few clubs get so organic a start
as this: originally Mod Club was
a weekly DJ series about town,
trafficking in Britpop and mod
revivalism with a loyal, elegantly
dress-appropriate following. Today
it's arguably Toronto's premier
mid-size concert venue, with top-
notch sound, video and lighting, and
nary a bad sightline. Programming
alternates between international
touring acts, in-the-know DJ nights
and local artists on the cusp of
bigger things (it's the venue where
Toronto's superstar The Weeknd
played his 2011 emergence gig).
722 College Street, M6G 1C5
+ 1 416 588 4663
themodclub.com

Four more music venues

01 Danforth Music Hall, The
Danforth: The Danforth's
interior features seating on
the upper balcony, while
its main floor conveniently
slants toward the stage for
general admission, creating
a social and convivial
atmosphere and an
acoustically sublime space.
thedanforth.com

02 The Silver Dollar Room,
Chinatown: This venue
has been a strip club,
jazz and blues joint and
all-around colourful player
in Toronto's music scene
for many years.
silverdollarroom.com

03 Air Canada Centre,
Entertainment District:
This is where music's big
names come when they're
in town. From Justin Bieber
and Bruce Springsteen to
Kanye West, the home of
the Toronto Maple Leafs
welcomes the great and the
good of international music.
theaircanadacentre.com

04 Massey Hall, Yonge-
Dundas: This 2,753-seat
venue hosts everything
from rock and pop to
country. Despite its
grand Palladian-revival
exterior and ornate
Moorish-revival interior,
the theatre's true design
triumph is its acoustics.
masseyhall.com

Media
Now see, hear

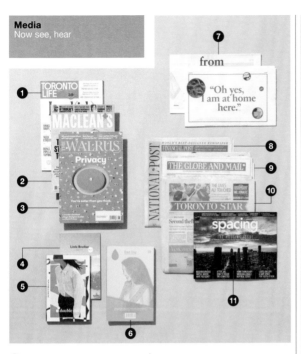

① Newspapers and magazines
Read all about it

Toronto isn't just Canada's cultural and financial capital, it's one of North America's liveliest and most competitive media markets.

With excellent reporting and commentary, city magazine ❶ *Toronto Life* distils the current mood of the city into one attractive package each month. News magazine ❷ *Maclean's* impresses with its national and international analysis, or for Canada's equal to *The New Yorker* or *Harper's* there's ❸ *The Walrus*. The always engaging ❹ *Little Brother*, produced by editor Emily M. Keeler and her designer partner Charles Yao, publishes many of Canada's best emerging literary writers, while every issue of ❺ *Double Dot* explores the cultural and creative relationship between a pair of sister cities. Culture zine ❻ *Bad Day* has been called "Toronto's little book of cool" and for an insider's take on the city's contemporary arts, pick up ❼ *Carbon Paper*.

The conservative ❽ *National Post* is strong on financial reporting, and for top-notch columnists and international newa there's ❾ *Globe and Mail*, which fancies itself as the country's paper of record. You'll find the city's diversity best reflected in the pages of the ❿ *Toronto Star* broadsheet, the country's highest-circulation daily, which still lives up to the progressive principles on which it was founded. Curious local favourite ⓫ *Spacing* is the model that every urban-affairs magazine should aspire to.

The Monocle Daily
It would be remiss not to mention Monocle 24's own radio show that offers a round-up of world news with a focus on the Americas. Our Toronto bureau and correspondents across the region will ensure that you stay completely up to date. *monocle.com/radio*

Radio

The crown-owned national radio and television broadcaster, the Canadian Broadcasting Corporation, is headquartered in Toronto. But all across the dial and online, the city boasts a packed radio environment in a Babel-esque variety of tongues.

01 CBC Radio One 99.1: The national broadcaster's local flagship news, current affairs and entertainment station. *Metro Morning*, hosted by Matt Galloway, is Toronto's most listened to morning show. *cbc.ca/radio*

02 Canadaland: A strong, listener-supported podcast network created by Jesse Brown, with regular programmes covering arts, politics and media criticism. *canadalandshow.com*

03 Chin Radio 91.9: Launched in 1966 by Johnny Lombardi, Chin is a pioneer of multilingual broadcasting, with programming in more than two-dozen languages. *chinradio.com*

04 Q: This is the most popular arts radio-programme in Canada. Despite a rocky few years it continues to attract the biggest names in music, film, the visual arts and media. *cbc.ca/radio/q*

05 Indie88: This new upstart station broadcasts out of a studio in the Liberty Village neighbourhood and has an emphasis on indie rock and emerging local artists. *Indie88.com*

Design and architecture
── Building excitement

There's no end to the architectural flourishes that adorn Toronto. From grand beaux arts and brutalist monuments to cosy Victorian homes and shimmering skyscrapers, the city's physical infrastructure and embellishments have much to say about its historical legacy.

In this chapter we have listed design landmarks both big and small. Some, including Union Station, betray Toronto's lofty ambitions at the turn of the 20th century when the city aspired towards Parisian grandeur. Others, such as the Financial District's Design Exchange, repurpose historic buildings while retaining their distinct architectural heritage.

In the warmer months, Torontonians love nothing more than to find a sunny patch of green to relax, so we also nominate the well-designed outdoor spaces where you can do just that. Read on to discover our favourite spots in the city.

Brutalist
Concrete classics

Smoke sign
The chimneys of the heating plant are a feature

1
University of Toronto Scarborough
Soft centre

In the early 1960s Australian architect John Andrews designed this kilometre-long facility set amid the lush greenery of the nearby Highland Creek valley. The project became a standout example of Canadian brutalism and modernist architecture.

The tiered, oblong building is crowned with a distinctive row of three chimneys. Austerity overload is avoided indoors in the classrooms and common areas through the use of terracotta-tile flooring and wooden panelling that infuse a sense of warmth.
1265 Military Trail, M1C 1A4

2
Massey College, Downtown
Study in tranquillity

Ron Thom was one of Canada's greatest modernist architects and many consider Massey College the Canadian zenith of the style. Taking cues from medieval colleges in Oxford and Cambridge as well as Arts and Crafts, Thom built red-brick buildings around a single quadrangle for this residential college for graduate students. The buildings block off the surrounding streets, so the atmosphere here is meditative – there's even a fish pond and water fountains. The courtyard clock tower houses the St Catherine bell that chimes at meal times.
4 Devonshire Place, M5S 2E1

④
Medical Sciences Building,
Discovery District
Showing its stripes

When Peter Goering completed
this building in 1969 it was known
for its simplicity and smooth
finishes and stood in stark contrast
to the older structures around it.
Later, when the building required
reinforcement, artists Ted Bieler
and Robert Downing found an
aesthetically innovative solution:
adorning the exteriors with random
panels of pre-cast concrete. The
cladding hides unsightly steel
supports and its distinct look has
led to the building's nickname:
the Shaggy Dog (the horizontal
embellishments look like long fur).
1 King's College Circle, M5S 1A8

③
Robarts Library, Downtown
Fully booked

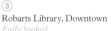

Robarts Library, the 1973-built
brutalist brainchild of firm Mathers
& Haldenby, is a gargantuan
14-storey block of concrete that
houses the University of Toronto's
book collection. Despite its hard
appearance it has a rather soft
nickname – the Peacock – thanks
to the resemblance it bears to the
bird. The Thomas Fisher Rare
Book Library forms the body, with
the main building appearing as a
fanned-out tail.

Umberto Eco, the Italian
author of *The Name of the Rose*,
was thought to have used Robarts
Library as the model for the library
depicted in his book.
130 St George Street, M5S 1A5

02

03

04

01

05

06   07

08

09 10

11

Reading material

Toronto's public libraries span more than a century, a journey best embodied by the Bloor/Gladstone branch, which fuses its 1913 heritage building with a glittering 2009 extension by RDH Architects. Further contrasts can be seen in Raymond Moriyama's mid-1970s scheme for the Toronto Reference Library and the efficient and adaptable interior of the city's 100th library at Scarborough Civic Centre.

The entryway to the Lillian H Smith Library features a mythical griffin and winged lion, a reference to its collection of rare sci-fi, fantasy and children's books. And visitors to the Fort York Library can see lines of poetry by famous Ontarian author Margaret Atwood threaded around its façade, enhanced by perforated fins featuring Charles Pachter art.
torontopubliclibrary.ca

01 — 03 Mount Dennis Library, York:
1123 Weston Road
+1 416 394 1008
04 — 05 Toronto Reference Library, Yorkville:
789 Yonge Street
+1 416 395 5577
06 — 07 Fort York Library, Fort York:
190 Fort York Boulevard
+1 416 393 6240
08 Lillian H Smith Library, Downtown:
239 College Street
+1 416 393 7746
09 Bloor/Gladstone Library, Dufferin Grove:
1101 Bloor Street West
+1 416 393 7674
10 — 11 Scarborough Civic Centre Library, Scarborough:
156 Borough Drive
+1 416 396 3599

Hall monitor
This is Toronto's fourth city hall

① Toronto City Hall, Queen Street West
Hall of fame

The astonishing, telenovela-like saga of the Rob Ford mayoralty wasn't the way most Torontonians would have chosen to receive global headlines. But they may have secretly enjoyed seeing their iconic city hall, the stage for many of Ford's follies, so prominently on display.

It is said that the design by Finnish architect Viljo Revell was almost consigned to the scrap heap. Initially rejected by the other judges overseeing the design competition, Revell's model was plucked from the discard pile by Eero Saarinen.

Two sculptural towers of different heights cradle the flying-saucer-like structure that houses the council chambers and seems to hover above a two-storey plinth. At the time of its inauguration people were a little unsure what to make of its avant-garde design, but as Toronto's confidence has surged they've come to embrace Revell's building as the symbol of their city.
100 Queen Street West, M5H 2N2
+1 416 392 2489
toronto.ca

② Sony Centre for the Performing Arts, Financial District
Change of tack

Born into the cultural turbulence of the early 1960s, the city's first modernist concert hall was a break from tradition. Designed by Earle C Morgan and Peter Dickinson, its low-lying geometrical structure is still striking. "It reminds me of an epic ocean liner," says CEO Mark Hammond. "That extraordinary cantilevered canopy as its prow, the terraces on either side [sadly one is now lost] representing the wake it leaves." Inside, York Wilson's mural "The Seven Lively Arts" represents Toronto's dynamic arts scene.
1 Front Street East, M5E 1B2
+1 416 368 6161
sonycentre.ca

③ Design Exchange, Financial District
Shares in creativity

Built in 1937 by architects George & Moorehouse and S H Maw, this was the home of Toronto's stock exchange until the institution moved out in 1983. Declared a heritage building, it was preserved while an office block was built around and over it, and is now the unlikely choice for Canada's first museum of design. But the art deco building has retained something of its original use. "We're still a place for exchange," says Shauna Levy, the museum's president and CEO, "but now ideas, innovation and education are the currency."
234 Bay Street, M5K 1B2
+1 416 363 6121
dx.org

④
Exhibition Place, Niagara
Architectural melting pot

The expansive lakefront grounds
of Exhibition Place, established in
1879, host a wide range of events,
from professional football games
to trade shows and fairs. Strikingly,
this diversity of function is
mirrored in its mix of architecture:
art deco, beaux arts, modern and
postmodern. It's even home to the
city's oldest residence, Scadding
Cabin. Look out for the Allstream
Centre (formerly the Automotive
Building): in 2009 its interior
underwent significant renovations,
transforming it from an open shell
into a conference centre true to its
art deco exterior.

The Carillon Tower, built in the
Netherlands and presented to the
city in 1974, is another must-see.
Essentially a 26-metre-high musical
instrument, it's home to 50 bells of
varying sizes and is one of just 11
such towers in the country.
100 Princes' Boulevard, M6K 3C3
+1 416 263 3064
explace.on.ca

Liquid assets
—
The plant
takes its water
from Lake
Ontario

⑤
RC Harris Water Treatment
Plant, Scarborough
Treat yourself

Unofficially known as the Palace
of Purification, this plant atop a
hill in the city's east end is both
a critical piece of infrastructure
(it still handles about 40 per
cent of Toronto's water supply)
and a much-admired piece of
architecture.

Completed in 1941 and named
after the longtime public works
commissioner who oversaw
its construction, the plant was
designed to incorporate an unlikely
degree of opulence. It's composed
of brick and limestone, with arched
windows and copper roofing, and
its cavernous marble hallways are
ornamented with mosaics and
touches of gleaming brass.

While the grounds can always
be visited, tours of the interior are
rare, so keep an eye out for special
occasions such as Doors Open
Toronto, during which landmark
buildings are opened to the public.
2701 Queen Street East, M4E 1H4

⑥
Sunnyside Pavilion, Sunnyside
Quiet beauty

The concrete Sunnyside Pavilion
provides a striking contrast to the
natural beauty of Humber Bay.
Architect Alfred H Chapman
designed it in 1922 as a changing
facility for the nearby beach and
for the adjacent swimming pool
(then the world's largest outdoor
pool) that was opened three years
later. Today it is home to a small
summer café and public courtyard,
and despite its proximity to the
Gardiner Expressway it's a
serene spot that feels miles from
the hustle and bustle of the city.
1755 Lake Shore Boulevard
West, M6S 5A3
+1 416 531 2233
sunnysidepavilion.com

⑦
Union Station,
Entertainment District
Building in transit

Erected in 1927, this beaux arts
edifice is being transformed from
the nation's largest transit node
into a civic space in its own right.
Toronto architecture and design firm
Partisans is part of the team working
on the revitalisation, which will see
new dining, shopping and cultural
spaces. "We were committed to
showing off the building's systems,"
says co-founder Alex Josephson.
   The project is due for
completion in 2019; in the
meantime the cavernous great
hall and 22 Doric limestone
columns fronting the façade
remain accessible to the public.
65 Front Street West, M5J 1E6

⑧
Distillery District
Vintage stuff

Founded in 1832, Gooderham and
Worts was little more than a windmill
on the lake. By 1887 it was the
world's largest distillery and today its
remnants form the largest collection
of Victorian industrial architecture
in North America. But the
Distillery District is no museum.
   Since 2003, under the Cityscape
Development Corporation, new
life has been breathed into the site,
with shops, artisans, restaurants,
theatres and contemporary art. The
buildings were designed in the 19th
century by father-and-son architects
David Roberts Sr and Jr and lend
atmosphere to the summer patios
and Christmas markets.
thedistillerydistrict.com

Winter Stations

With temperatures dipping
as low as minus 40C during
winter, Torontonians prefer to
huddle indoors by a fireplace.
The Winter Stations, however,
provide a good reason to go
out and brave the elements.
About a dozen or so of these
public art installations – chosen
in an international competition
– are brought to life along
Toronto's beaches from
February to March, with
visitors welcome to engage
with the interactive structures.
The outdoor showcase was
first introduced in 2015 and
each year the works on show
address a different theme.
winterstations.com

Towers
Architectural high points

① CN Tower, Entertainment District
Inspiring spire

This is the city's most visited attraction and the one building you definitely won't miss. Completed in 1976 and topping out at 553 metres, for more than 30 years this communications tower was the world's tallest freestanding structure (a reign ended by Dubai's Burj Khalifa in 2009). The tower has a sculptural elegance and was named one of the seven modern wonders of the world by the American Society of Civil Engineers.

The views from the Observation Deck are exhilarating, whether you're witnessing the painterly compositions of light and shadow over Lake Ontario or watching the miniaturised city below, going about its business like a real-life *Sim City*. If you're in need of thrills you can even step outside – tethered, of course – and walk the tower's circumference.
301 Front Street West, M5V 2T6
+1 416 868 6937
cntower.ca

② Royal Bank Plaza, Financial District
Gold standard

Completed in 1976 and 1979 respectively, Royal Bank Plaza's North and South towers were created when the Royal Bank of Canada moved headquarters from Montréal to Toronto. Their golden sheen emanates from 14,000, 24-carat windows; the thin layer of gold is decorative but also functions as insulation.

The beauty of these buildings goes deeper than flashy façades, however. The skeletal structures on a triangular footprint brilliantly stagger the curtain wall system; the resulting jagged bays and piers reflect the city around them in a dizzying mosaic.
200 Bay Street, M5J 2J2

③ Manufacturers Life Insurance Building, Yorkville
Classy and grassy

This formidable Indiana limestone structure was built by Toronto architects Henry Sproatt and Ernest Ross Rolph in the beaux arts style in 1926. Marani & Morris architects crowned the structure with additional offices in 1953, their more modern and pared-down aesthetic creating a pillared rooftop balcony to mirror the columns at the building's base. But it's the lawn that captures a lot of attention at street level, says architectural historian Sharon Vattay. "It looks like a green well-vacuumed carpet for most of the year."
200 Bloor Street East, M4W 1E5

Grand design
———

In the 1920s, the plan was for University Avenue to be a boulevard of stately buildings. While it was never fully realised, one grand structure was: the Canada Life Building. The beaux arts edifice has the symmetry and authority of classicism on a larger scale.

I'll race you to the top, Papachan... On your marks, get set... go!

④

Toronto-Dominion Centre,
Financial District
Tall storeys

The first tower of the Toronto-
Dominion Centre opened in 1967,
marking the beginning of the age
of the city's skyscrapers. Designed
by architect Ludwig Mies van der
Rohe, it was unlike anything the
city had seen before (one politician
at the time called it "orange-crate
architecture"). The stark matt-
black steel of its six towers spans
56 storeys, accentuated by floor-to-
ceiling bronzed windows.
77 King Street West, M5K 2A1
+1 416 304 1953
tdcentre.com

Residential buildings
Living history

High numbers
—
Prii built 250 such whimsical buildings in Toronto

(1)

Jane Exbury Towers, North York
Eye-catching curves

Estonian Uno Prii migrated to Toronto in 1950 to launch a career erecting more than a dozen residential high-rises. While modernism was his starting point, his method departed from the style's characteristic straight lines and replaced them with sweeping curves. It was a bold approach that infuriated some but commissions kept rolling in, including the Jane Exbury Towers. The unique profile of the five 20-storey residential blocks, completed in 1969, was described by a reporter as a "spirited break in the skyline" – an assessment that still holds true today.

2415 Jane Street, M3M 1A9

I'll call this one 'Building a Better Life'

The growth of wood

While you may notice that red-brick and stucco top the list of materials favoured in the construction of new Toronto houses, it's worth acknowledging the recent rise in the use of timber too – a trend that reflects an increase in environmental awareness. Architects Christopher Glaisek and Kyra Clarkson of Modernest are two such champions of this return to natural materials. Their homes are inspired by classic modernism, with exteriors featuring black Douglas fir in a patchwork arrangement to accentuate the wood's grain and texture. Inside, solid-wood flooring evokes warmth and personality.
modernest.ca

**Palmerston Boulevard,
The Annex**
Grand scheme

With its large detached houses,
cast-iron, glass-globe street
lamps and wider road (24 metres,
compared to 20 elsewhere),
everything about Palmerston
Boulevard is grander than its
counterparts elsewhere in the city.

Make your way in via the stone
gate near Bathurst and Bloor
streets (this was once a gated
community) and as you wander,
keep an eye out for number 469.
This brick residence with its airy
verandas was built in 1906 by
George Weston, who founded
a bread company that would
eventually expand to become
Canada's largest private-sector
employer, owning grocery chain
Loblaws and pharmacist Shoppers
Drugmart. Unfortunately the
house has since been divided
into apartments – a sad fate that
has also befallen many of its
neighbours on the boulevard.

Parks
Green spaces

Guild Park, Scarborough
Sculpture club

Set above the Scarborough Bluffs
and measuring nearly 36 hectares
in area, Guild Park consists of both
gardens and forest. It's also home
to 12 sculptures "preserved from
more than 50 heritage buildings
now demolished", says John
Mason, president of the Friends
of Guild Park. The Friends put
on guided walks around the park
so you can get a better idea of
the works and their provenance;
Mason's own favourite is the Greek
Theatre, designed by Canadian
modernist architect Ron Thom,
who repurposed marble columns
from a century-old bank.
*201 Guildwood Parkway, M1P 4N7
guildpark.ca*

**Trinity Bellwoods Park,
Trinity Bellwoods**
Bring a blanket

The stone-and-iron gates on
Queen Street West are the only
remnants of the 19th-century
college that gave this park its
name. Today it's one of the city's
most cherished places to spend
long summer days on a blanket
with a cold drink. It's packed on
weekends, when it can be nearly
impossible to find a spot; for peace
and quiet try the less populated
Dundas Street West side, also host to
a Tuesday farmers' market between
May and October. Carolyn Wong,
one of its founders, says the market,
like the park, "is very laidback".
*790 Queen Street West, M6J 1G3
trinitybellwoods.ca*

Kew Gardens, The Beaches
Waterfront walk

Kew Gardens is the crown jewel
of The Beaches, Toronto's lakefront
community. The park stretches
from the Queen Street East
commercial strip down to the
water, making it the perfect entry
point to the boardwalk and the long
sandy stretches by the lake.

Friends of the Beach Parks
keeps the area active with
events and plantings and is also
responsible for maintaining the
Kew Community Fireplace. On
the beach side of the park, this
is lit every Friday night and
weekend afternoons from mid-
December to March.
2075 Queen Street East, M4E 2N9

Visual identity
The look of the city

2
Path logo, Financial District
Pointing the way

Scattered around the city are more than 125 posts sporting this colourful logo. Designed in 1988 by two agencies, Gottschalk + Ash International and Keith Muller, the signs mark entry points to Path, the world's largest underground shopping complex. Its 30km of subterranean passages connect 370,000 sq m of retail space, more than 50 buildings, and landmarks such as the CN Tower, the Rogers Centre and Roy Thomson Hall. It's a comfortable way to get around in the brutal winter months and the logo provides directions: the red P tells you you're going south, the orange A points west, the blue T is north and the yellow H shows east.

1
Little Free Libraries, citywide
Loan arrangers

Torontonians love their libraries (*see page 108*). With 100 neighbourhood branches, the city's public system is the busiest, by number of books borrowed, in the world. But it seems even that isn't enough to sate people's appetite for reading. Spend some time walking residential streets and you're likely to spot a front lawn sporting a birdhouse-like structure filled with volumes. A note encourages passers-by to "Take a book, leave a book."

Though the movement behind these Little Free Libraries didn't originate in Toronto, locals have embraced the idea of book-sharing hobbit houses with enthusiasm. The collections can be surprisingly good; rather than use them as bins for ratty, unwanted paperbacks, residents are motivated by the desire to share their passion for great reads. They also tend to perk up a street, akin to drawing strangers together at the neighbourhood water cooler.

Manholes
———
It's easy to gaze up and marvel at many great landmarks but sometimes it's worth looking down too. Countless manhole covers dot the city's roads. The iron chequered grid design was the brainchild of Toronto's first official photographer, Arthur Goss, in 1910.

③ Trams, citywide
Streetcars to desire

While most cities spent the postwar years tearing up tram lines to make way for more cars, Toronto maintained what would become an integral, more environmentally friendly piece of public infrastructure.

Today the trams (known in North America as streetcars) are an iconic presence on neighbourhood high streets and in the vertiginous chasms of Downtown. Locals may grumble about overcrowding in rush hours but for visitors they're more than just a convenient way to get around: they're a way to better appreciate the city at street level.

The current stock of streetcars is being replaced by handsome, low-level, articulated cars built by Bombardier. Even better, a couple of the system's original vintage models are going back into limited circulation. Known affectionately as "Red Rockets", their design dates back to the 1930s.

④ Crosswalks, citywide
Press, look, point

These pedestrian crossings have been helping Torontonians get to the other side of the road safely since 1958. The original version – white stripes and signs saying "Pedestrian X crossing" and "Stop for Pedestrians" – proved not to be very successful, with a pedestrian fatality logged on their very first day of use.

Adjustments were swiftly made to enhance their effectiveness. The original white was removed in favour of a more visible amber and illustrations were added to instruct pedestrians to press, look and point. The crossings were also outfitted with flashing lights so that drivers would be able to spot them at night.

Thanks for the ride! It would have been a long walk with a bird on my head

⑤ Graffiti Alley, Queen Street West
Playing tag

Tucked away in a warren of back alleys just south of Queen Street West, and running between Portland and Spadina, you'll find this sprawling, semi-legit showcase for the city's street artists. It's a rolling tableau of elaborate, building-sized murals that changes with some frequency, the artists taking their cues from hip-hop culture, op-art, Japanese anime and more besides.

The kilometre-long strip rose in prominence when Torontonian satirist Rick Mercer chose it as the location for his weekly monologue on his TV show *The Mercer Report*. *Rush Lane, M5V 2W1*

Sport and fitness
—— Work it out

Toronto is an active place despite the deep freeze of the winter months and the sweltering heat of summer. There are plenty of opportunities to be on the move no matter what the weather's up to. Its excellent rowing and sailing clubs make the most of the city's lakeside location, while on land you can sign up for a scenic jog with one of Toronto's most dedicated running clubs. And when things do turn chilly you can visit a legendary Toronto boxing gym for a session with a genuine heavyweight champ or tackle the walls in a cutting-edge climbing centre.

And when it's time to wind down after your exertions? We've listed the best options for a pampering hair trim.

Outdoor options
Fresh air and fitness

①
Argonaut Rowing Club, Liberty Village
Totally oarsome

Founded by members of the UK's Oxford and Cambridge rowing associations in 1872, this is one of the country's oldest rowing clubs (check out the trophies dating back to the 1800s), and has sent more crews to the Olympics than any other Canadian club. It's located on Lake Ontario, with a rowing channel that extends 4.5km to the Humber River, and offers lessons for all skill levels. If you're an early bird, take an hour-long class at sunrise – the view of the skyline is breathtaking.
1225 Lakeshore Boulevard West, M6K 3C1
+ 1 416 532 2803
argonautrowingclub.com

Rowing's not my strong suit. But I'll watch from the sidelines with a cocktail...

Keep calm
A long wall ensures the water stays flat for rowing

②

Parkdale Roadrunners, Parkdale
Hit the road

Started by a few friends in 2010, this west-end running community attracts dozens of runners of all ages and abilities every Tuesday night. "We felt a responsibility to give back to the community we run through," says co-founder Steven Artemiw. Runs begin at the Gladstone Hotel, with a women-only session on Saturday mornings.

The group also hosts track workouts and longer runs. The well-known Parkdale Roadrunners singlets, along with the group's cheering section, are fixtures at Toronto's two annual marathons, as well as the dozens of other road races held throughout the year.
parkdaleroadrunners.com

Island life
—
Toronto Island is a short ferry ride from Downtown and is an ideal getaway from the bustle of the city. We recommend a cycle or a jog along its winding paths, then a session soaking up the sun on its many beaches for the perfect (summer) day trip.

③
Harbourfront Centre Sailing
& Powerboating, Harbourfront
Ahoy there

Once an industrial wasteland,
Toronto's waterfront has become
the perfect starting point from
which to explore Lake Ontario
and the dozens of lagoons and
marinas around Toronto Island.
Harbourfront Centre Sailing &
Powerboating has more than 30
courses and some 90 boats for rent,
including sailing boats, yachts and
dinghies. Speedboats are available
too, no experience required; just
remember your driver's licence.
Bring a picnic to enjoy on the island
before you head back to the city.
235 Queens Quay West, M5J 2G8
+1 416 973 4000
harbourfrontcentre.com/boating

Indoor options
Undercover exercising

❶
Sully's Boxing Gym,
Dovercourt Park
It's a knockout

Walk up the stairs inside Sully's
Boxing Gym, opened in 1943 by
Earl "Sully" Sullivan, and the first
thing you'll notice is the collection
of photographs, yellowed vintage
posters of past boxing contests
and cut-outs of the sport's greats
hanging from the walls.
    This is the most fabled boxing
gym in Toronto. The equipment may
not be state of the art but the friendly
trainers will work you through
manoeuvres such as weighted squats,
jumping stacked tyres and scaling
flights of stairs, as well as, of course,
a few rounds on the punchbags.
    "Lennox Lewis, Muhammad
Ali: they've all been through here,"
says Tony Morrison (*pictured*), a
trainer at the gym and former light
heavyweight champion. In the back
they have the baseboard for the
speedbag Ali used to train with.
1024 Dupont Street, M6H 1Z6
+1 416 805 8108
sullysboxinggym.com

Ice, ice baby
———
Curling lacks ice hockey's
glamour but Canada's third
sport is still a quietly absorbing
pursuit. As befits its genteel
image, it has eschewed brash
commercialism: most of its
athletes have day jobs. Visit
Toronto's Royal Canadian
Curling Club for a match.
rccc.on.ca

Old warhorses
—
Canadian troops trained here for war

(2)
Riding Academy, Liberty Village
Saddle up

In June 2003 the Riding Academy opened in the heart of the grand Exhibition Place. The country's best equestrian facility is housed in the 1931 Horse Palace (one of Canada's finest art deco buildings) and offers best-in-class coaching, a 15-horse stable and certified hunter-jumper and dressage specialists. "It has the ambience of a bygone era," says managing director Sue Iwan, "and the magic of a stable full of history and memories." Call to book a lesson. In November the academy is one of the venues for the Royal Agricultural Winter Fair.
15 Nova Scotia Avenue, M6K 3L3
+1 416 599 4044
horsepalace.ca

Five national sports

01 Ice hockey
Canada is praised for its liberal, tolerant values and yet its national sport is a raucous, often violent affair. Go figure. Better still, go see some ice hockey in fast-and-furious action, courtesy of the Toronto Maple Leafs at Downtown's Air Canada Centre. The season is from October to April.
mapleleafs.nhl.com

02 Baseball
US sport fans might claim it as their own but baseball has a passionate following here, notably the exploits of the Blue Jays, who in the early 1990s became the only non-US team to win a World Series. The season lasts from April to October.
toronto.bluejays.mlb.com

03 Basketball
Whether basketball was, as some claim, invented by an Ontarian, the sport's big here and its finest practitioners are the NBA-ranked Raptors. The season is October to April.
nba.com/raptors

04 Soccer
The city's top soccer team, Toronto FC was started in 2007, coinciding with a growth in popularity of the sport. The team plays at BMO Field from March to October.
torontofc.ca

05 Curling
Imported to Canada by Scottish immigrants, curling is where to go after the adrenaline buzz of hockey. The sport involves two teams of four players pushing a granite stone across the ice, similar to a giant game of shuffleboard. It's played from August to April.
torontocurling.com

③
City Dance Corps, Chinatown
Moving experience

The old adage says that it takes two to tango but Estelle Nicol and Tina Nico, who opened these studios in 2002, have demonstrated that there's no upper limit. There are more than 160 classes per week and 45 instructors specialising in everything from hip-hop and jazz to aerial silks and tango. High windows and whitewashed brick walls give the place a romantic feel. With drop-in classes every day, even those with the tightest of schedules will find something to tap their toes to.
489 Queen Street West, M5V 2B4
+1 416 260 2356
citydancecorps.com

Basecamp Climbing, Christie Pits
Rising excitement

Basecamp boasts 12-metre-high walls, 650 sq m of climbing space and more than 100 routes to choose from in a site that was formerly an adult cinema. The cutting-edge gym also offers lessons that cater to all skill levels – from first-timers through to seasoned climbers – and the routes are changed every month so you'll rarely repeat one. Established by owner Matthew Languay in February 2016, it is the tallest indoor climbing arena in Downtown. It's conveniently located too, with Christie subway station just across the road.
677 Bloor Street West, M6G 1L3
+1 416 855 0430
basecampclimbing.ca

①
Glassbox, Little Italy
Quality not quantity

Customers are sure to feel well taken care of in this barbershop run by owners Dylan Portner and Peter Gosling. Arriving at the bright, simple shop, you'll be offered something to drink and if it's a busy day – reassuringly the stylists here like to take their time over individual cuts – there's a pool table and colourful artworks by Toronto artists to keep you amused.

Grooming
A cut above

A fine collection of grooming products includes pomades and beard oils from the US and Canada.
338 Harbord Street, M6G 1H2
+1 416 516 6237
glassboxbarbershop.com

②
Fuss Hair Studio, Leslieville
It's all in the details

As its name might suggest, everything about Fuss has been considered meticulously. "Some people say it's just hair," says Kristin Rankin, who started the company with Stacey Lipstein in 2008. "It's not; it's somebody's identity." In 2015 it became the first salon in Toronto to charge gender-neutral rates, celebrating the city's famed egalitarianism.
Located in Leslieville, it's one of a group of salons giving the city's west-end equivalents a run for their money. "We could feel that the area was about to catch fire," says Rankin.
1093 Queen Street East, M4M 1L7
+1 416 469 0006
fusshairstudio.com

The art of cycling
——
Art Spin began in 2009 offering bicycle tours of Toronto's galleries, and has since developed into a grassroots cultural force, commissioning projects with the aim of producing artwork outside the gallery context. Oh, and it still runs popular bike tours.
artspin.ca

I tried out for the Niagara IceDogs but they wouldn't let me on the team...

(3)

Garrison's By The Park,
Niagara Village
Personal best

Garrison's fits with the city's
other modish barbershops – the
subway-tile walls, the tattooed
thirty-somethings at their stations –
but when it comes to old-fashioned
customer service, it stands apart.
"It's a personal thing, getting your
hair cut," says barber Jared Quast.
"We get that."

With a talented team and product
line including Layrite Pomade and
Kleinburg-based Crown Shaving,
founders Doug Stewart and Hollis
Hopkins take a clear stand on
quality. Booking is essential.
254 Niagara Street, M6J 2L8
+ 1 416 703 8602
garrisons.ca

Cycling routes
Pedal power

(1)

Martin Goodman Trail,
Harbourfront
Scenic views

STARTING POINT:
Harbourfront Centre
DISTANCE: 17km (round trip)

Start on Toronto's Downtown
waterfront, which has been
transformed in recent years into a
well-used and vibrant stretch of the
city. Head west along Queens Quay
West from ❶ *Harbourfront Centre*
until the road ends at Stadium Road
and joins with the Waterfront Trail.

Here follow the trail north, then
left into ❷ *Coronation Park* where
it merges with the most scenic
section of the Martin Goodman
Trail. Keep going past the oaks that
were planted to honour Canada's
war veterans. Leaving the park
you'll notice on your right the
❸ *Exhibition Place* building, home
to one of the largest fairs in North
America: the 1879 Canadian
National Exhibition.

Continue west to the
❹ *Humber Bay Arch Bridge*,
about 8.5km from your starting
point. Stop here to take in the views
before heading back. If you still
have the energy, take the Humber
River Recreational Trail route
(about 3km) to the 100-year-old
stone bridge at the Old Mill Road;
check directions before setting off.
It starts in the South Humber Park,
200 or so metres north from the
Humber Bridge.

Martin Goodman Trail

Humber Bay

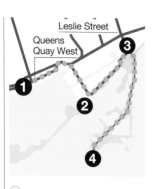

(2)

Leslie Street Spit, Harbourfront
Wild ride

STARTING POINT:
Harbourfront Centre
DISTANCE: 11km

This route takes you east to
Tommy Thompson Park, Toronto's
massive urban wilderness park and
de facto bird sanctuary, which is
open to the public on weekends.
Known as the Leslie Street Spit,
the man-made peninsula stretches
5km into Lake Ontario, wrapping
around Toronto Island and offering
sweeping views. On Saturday and
Sunday, birdwatchers mix with
joggers and cyclists to enjoy the
wide-open space.

Pick up a short-term rental
bike from any of the Bike Share
Toronto racks Downtown, or – for
something a little faster – choose
from the selection of hybrid and
road bikes from Gears in the Canary
District. Start at the ❶ *Harbourfront
Centre* then head east along the
Martin Goodman Trail. After about
2.7km you'll reach Cherry Street.
Veer right and follow the bike path
over the Don River through the
Port Lands industrial area until
you reach the sands of ❷ *Cherry
Beach*. From there, follow the trail
northeast to where it ends at the
marina, and then wind around
Unwin Avenue until you find the
gates of ❸ *Tommy Thompson Park*.

Head south along the paved
trail (minding out for a few speed
bumps) and one short footbridge
where you will have to walk your
bike. Pack a picnic to enjoy at the
automated ❹ *lighthouse* at the end
of your ride.

Running routes
Pound the pavement

①
St Lawrence Market
Snack run

DISTANCE: 6km
GRADIENT: Mostly flat
DIFFICULTY: Easy
SURFACE: Road, cobblestone
HIGHLIGHT: The view of the skyline from Sugar Beach
BEST TIME: Saturday morning, for the farmers' market
NEAREST SUBWAY: King

Start at the north end of St Lawrence Market, Toronto's central marketplace since 1803. Head down Lower Jarvis Street towards Lake Ontario. Run beneath the highway and cross Queen's Quay. By the water, to your left, you'll find the umbrellas at Sugar Beach. With the Downtown skyline on your left, follow Dockside Drive east to Sherbourne Common. Go further east along the Martin Goodman Trail to Parliament Street and pass north under the highway once again.

On your left note Tom Longboat Lane, named after a First Nations runner who, while representing Canada in 1907, set the course record at the Boston Marathon. Take the cobblestone-surfaced Gristmill Lane on your right to pass through the Distillery Historic District. A left on Trinity Street takes you to Mill Street. Head east on Mill Street and cross Cherry Street, into the new Canary District. Skirt around the edge of 7.3-hectare Corktown Common, which borders the Don River.

Cross Bayview Avenue to Underpass Skate Park, home to some of the city's finest graffiti murals. Head up to King Street and turn left. Head west, then keep left onto Cherry Street, back down to Mill Street. Head west again, crossing Parliament Square Park. Continue west along The Esplanade to St Lawrence Market itself. Fêted by some as one of the best food markets in North America, the market hall's 120 permanent sellers will have something for you to replenish energy stocks.

②
City Hall
Architecture tour

DISTANCE: 5.6km
GRADIENT: Slight incline, then flat
DIFFICULTY: Easy
SURFACE: Pavement, crushed gravel
HIGHLIGHT: Running around Queen's Park and seeing many of the city's architectural jewels
BEST TIME: Early morning
NEAREST SUBWAY: Osgoode or Queen

From Nathan Phillips Square head west past Osgoode Hall's black gates. Turn north onto University Avenue and continue past the hospitals and the Mars Discovery District, Toronto's start-up hub. Cross College Street toward the statue of John A MacDonald, Canada's first prime minister. Veer right along Queens Park Crescent East to pass the Legislative Assembly of Toronto, sculpted from pink sandstone quarried in Ontario.

At Wellesley Street enter the park and follow the paths straight north under the oak, pine and maple trees. Take the north exit onto Queens Park; head further north for about 200 metres up to Bloor Street. Turn left at the Royal Ontario Museum, after which, on your left, you'll find the gates to Philosopher's Walk. This opens onto the Toronto University's St George Campus. Follow Philosopher's Walk to Hoskin Avenue, then right at Trinity College and Trinity College Chapel. A few blocks west, in view of the Robarts Library towers, turn south onto St George Street.

With the CN Tower in front of you, continue south and turn right at Wilcocks Street. At Spadina Avenue, turn left to head south, via Spadina Crescent roundabout, to rejoin College Street. Head west and after a few blocks turn left into Kensington Market, down along Augusta Avenue. Refuel here at any of the jumble of juice shops, cafés and bakeries.

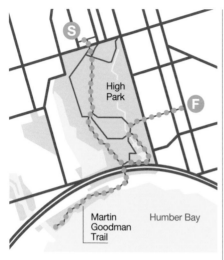

3 High Park
Green scene

DISTANCE: 6.4km
GRADIENT: Steep decline, then flat
DIFFICULTY: Hard
SURFACE: Pavement
HIGHLIGHT: Enjoying Toronto's green oasis, High Park
BEST TIME: Early morning, to enjoy the park to yourself
NEAREST SUBWAY: High Park

Begin at High Park subway station. From High Park Avenue, cross Bloor Street West and enter the park. Continue straight along Colborne Lodge Drive until you come to the fork in the road. Stay on the left on Colborne Lodge Drive until you reach the fork with West Road and head past High Park Zoo.

Continue straight as the road takes a steep decline. Exit the park and take care as you cross all three of the highways in front of you (using the pedestrian crossings): the Queensway, the Gardiner Expressway (via an underground tunnel), then Lake Shore Boulevard West. On the other side of these busy roads you'll find the Martin Goodman Trail. Turn right and wind around the shared bicycle and footpath until you have reached the white arches of the bridge over the mouth of the Humber River.

Turn back to retrace your steps, crossing the highways at the same points again on Colborne Lodge Drive to make your way back into the park. With the busy Queensway at your back, take the path on your right. After 500 or so metres you'll come across a pond; keep this on your right and run north to Spring Road. As Spring Road becomes Centre Road, hang a right and continue to High Park Boulevard. Cross under the stone gates and run east along the pavement to Roncesvalles Avenue. Here you can catch your breath at any of the charming coffee shops that line the street.

4 Kay Gardner Beltline Park
Quiet time

DISTANCE: 4km
GRADIENT: Steady climb
DIFFICULTY: Medium
SURFACE: Pavement, crushed gravel
HIGHLIGHT: It's a world away from busy Downtown
BEST TIME: Anytime
NEAREST SUBWAY: Davisville

Start just south of the Davisville subway station on Yonge Street. Look for the concrete stairs on your right; these lead up to the Kay Gardner Beltline Trail, a recreational route through uptown Toronto. Built on a former rail corridor, it heads by ravines and hidden green spaces.

Set out west, crossing the road on the old rail bridge. At several junctures you will have to cross over two-way roads to refind the trail so be sure to look both ways or use the crosswalks at the nearest traffic lights.

After about 3.5km you will be next to the Allen Road expressway. Follow the small path south beside the highway and find Eglinton West subway station, where you can zip back Downtown.

If you are feeling energetic, continue south 400 metres along Everden Road (opposite the station) into Cedarvale Park (opening hours are 08.00 to 23.00). There are numerous paths crossing this urban greenspace and it leads to impressive views of the Downtown skyline.

Where to buy
——
Mountain Equipment Co-op (*mec.ca*), Black Toe (*blacktoerunning.com*), The Running Room (*runningroom.com*) and Nike (*nike.ca*).

Walks
— Where to wander

Toronto's mosaic of neighbourhoods makes for an eminently walkable city. While one can spend days exploring new areas, we've whittled down the list to our favourite five, including the key landmarks, shops and restaurants to check out. Whether it's well-heeled Rosedale, grungy Kensington Market or village-esque Roncesvalles, each presents a distinct facet of what life looks like for the people who call Toronto home.

NEIGHBOURHOOD 01

Summerhill and Rosedale
Affluent and influential

Toronto's longest street, Yonge, sprouts north from Bloor Street, leaving the Financial District's dense mess of office skyscrapers and condominiums behind. In their place are the low-rise residences and independent shopfronts of Rosedale and Summerhill. Rosedale is named for the wild rose bushes once plentiful in the area, while Summerhill was christened after a stately 1842 manor built by Canadian businessman Charles Thompson, around which the neighbourhood developed. Sadly, the house was razed in 1913.

Among the city's most affluent residential neighbourhoods, the oldest architectural specimens sport extra sheen compared to their counterparts elsewhere. The area enjoys easy Downtown access and retains a certain bucolic charm thanks to the natural greenery and ravines, and the well-maintained 19th-century residences with their tidily manicured hedges. A walk through these parts is a survey of Toronto's best-preserved examples of Georgian revival, Tudor revival and art deco architecture.

Our trail takes you to some of the highlights of the area, including a host of the city's top businesses; here you'll find purveyors of everything from fashion and vintage furniture to cold-press juices. Be sure to choose appropriate footwear: the walk includes a section of nature trail too.

Yonge Street and parks tour
Summerhill and Rosedale walk

Start off with a brew at ❶ *Boxcar Social*, where residents have come since 2014 for their morning caffeine fix made from a rotating menu of beans from around the world.

Turn right as you leave, then take the first right onto Birch Avenue. A little way down on the right is ❷ *Wooftown*, with everything a dog could want. Grab a Hugglehound ragdoll for your pooch (if you have one), then retrace your steps and

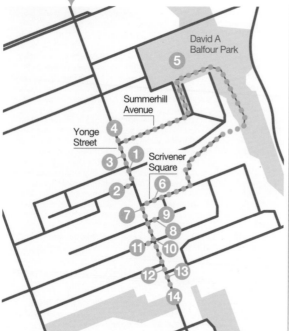

head past Boxcar Social. On your left you'll see ③ *Tuck Shop Trading Co*, Lyndsay Borschke's cosy shop that retails fashion and accessories made by Canadian creatives. Continue up the gentle slope to ④ *Room 2046*. Part shop, part coffee bar and part studio, there's always something to discover in its eclectic range, from sunglasses to coffee-table books.

As you leave, cross the road and head to the end of Summerhill Avenue. Take the path left before Summerhill Gardens and follow it to Rosehill Reservoir. From there cut across to ⑤ *David A Balfour Park*. Take time exploring the Vale of Avoca ravine, slowly making your way south; watch out for the Canadian Pacific Railway Bridge, your sign to re-enter the built environment on Mathersfield Drive.

Follow Mathersfield Drive and cross the playground at the end. Beyond, on your right, you'll see ⑥ *North Toronto Train Station*, an exemplar of beaux arts architecture and now home to the city's grandest liquor retailer. The 43-metre-high clock tower is less than half the size of its inspiration, the bell tower of St Mark's in Venice. Pass by and immediately in front of you will be Yonge Street and ⑦ *The Rosedale Diner*; it's served comfort food since 1978. Or if you're hankering after an Aperol Spritz turn left on Yonge Street for ⑧ *Terroni*. This Italian restaurant is one of the Five Thieves, the name residents have given the pricey line of food businesses that pride themselves on the quality of their offerings.

After lunch, peruse the racks at ⑨ *The Narwhal* next door on Price

Getting there

The walk's starting point at Boxcar Social is easily accessible. Turn right on Shaftesbury Avenue after exiting Summerhill subway station. The café is right across the road from Shaftesbury's intersection with Yonge Street.

Street. The womenswear boutique carries independent designers that are hard to find elsewhere in Toronto. Head back to Yonge Street and turn left; on the corner of Macpherson Avenue is ⑩ *Hopson Grace*, selling flatware and "joyful essentials" from crockery to tablecloths. Owners Andrea Hopson and Martha Grace McKimm aim to inspire your next meal with chic products.

Just down Macpherson Avenue is ⑪ *Greenhouse Juice Co*, stocked with cold-press fruit and vegetable concoctions. Grab a bottle and head right on Yonge Street, towards Rosedale. Nearly two blocks down is ⑫ *Want Apothecary*, the Toronto flagship of Montréal leather accessory designers Dexter and Byron Peart. At ⑬ *ShopNyLa* a couple doors along is a round-up of the latest from New York and LA's established and emerging designers.

Cross to the corner of Crescent Road and you can enjoy a decadent treat from the sandwich maestros at ⑭ *Black Camel*. Order the pulled-pork and head to Ramsden Park opposite. Find some shade and tuck in for the perfect end to the day.

NEIGHBOURHOOD 02

Kensington
Unchanging appeal

Wedged between College and Dundas streets to the north and south and flanked by Bathurst Street and Spadina Avenue, Kensington is centrally located but its homely atmosphere (founded, in part, on its multicultural roots) marks a contrast from the surrounding urban bustle.

While the neighbouring areas have changed dramatically over the past decades, Kensington has evolved more quietly. Originally home to Toronto's Jewish community, waves of immigration through the mid-20th century brought new people to the area. At its heart is the popular street market, a spread of retail outlets – including extensions and buildouts reaching the pavements – that is also its defining architectural feature.

In the summer, roads are frequently closed off to traffic on Sundays so visitors can experience Kensington in all its pedestrian glory. It's a lively mix of unexpected sights, smells and sounds. There are buskers and street-art fairs, coffee roasters and spice shops. It's a raucous gathering place for people from all over Toronto and beyond; a place where foreign cultures and subcultures collide.

Spanning about 10 city blocks in total, Kensington is highly walkable and that's certainly the best way to experience all this area has to offer.

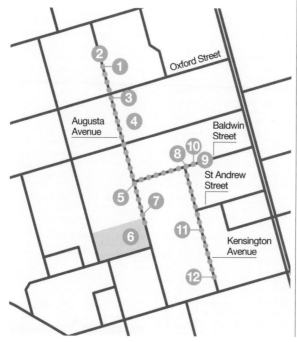

Market tour
Kensington walk

We recommend starting with an early coffee at neighbourhood favourite ❶ *Café Pamenar* while most of Kensington is still asleep. The market doesn't liven up until mid-morning, making Pamenar's back patio the perfect place to take in the calm with your first cup. Head south on Augusta Avenue. On your left after Oxford is ❷ *Model Citizen* (*see page 55*) with a great selection of menswear and

jewellery from Toronto designers. Time it right and you might even catch staff screen-printing their own line of T-shirts at the back. If you're peckish, grab a yoghurt bowl to go from ❸ *Grk Ygrt*, or cross Augusta Street and get pastries from Bunner's Bakeshop.

You'll come across ❹ *Good Egg*, a shop specialising in cookbooks and other food-related paraphernalia, a few shopfronts south. If you're in a giving mood, ❺ *Blue Banana Market* across the street has you covered for one-of-a-kind hand-crafted gifts. You can find anything from candles to platters and more kitschy items like moustache wax and printed socks.

Continue down Augusta for a few minutes until you pass Baldwin Street. On the east side of the street you'll see ❻ *Sweet Olenka's*, a necessary pit-stop, especially for ice cream if it's a hot day. Take your sweets a little way down the road and across the street to enjoy at ❼ *Bellevue Square Park*, the main gathering place in Kensington and home to picnics, drum circles and the odd Frisbee game.

When you're ready, across the street on Augusta is ⑧ *Kid Icarus* (*see page 63*), a stationery and gift shop specialising in handmade paper goods. Browse the cards, pads, and prints, most of which are made at the back of the shop.

Go back up Augusta Avenue and hang a right on Baldwin Street. Here you'll see everything from fishmonger's (Hooked) to butcher's (Sanagan's Meat Locker). Keep going until you hit the corner of Baldwin Street and Kensington Avenue. ⑨ *Torteria San Cosme* has some of the city's best Mexican sandwiches. Opt for a Pepito, a Latin take on the steak sandwich with meat from Sanagan's across the way.

Then continue down Baldwin Street. Your next stop is on the left: ⑩ *Wilbe Bloomin* plant shop. It's hard to miss: the pavement outside is usually covered in seasonal shrubs and flowers. Take time to smell the roses.

Head back the way you came and, just before the junction with Kensington Avenue, you should stop at ⑪ *Blackbird Baking Co*,

known for some of the best bread and desserts in the city. Its loaves are featured on menus in many restaurants in Toronto so be sure to pick one up for later.

Turn left down Kensington Avenue and walk a few blocks. This is the heart of the market; here you'll find grocery and produce stalls mixed in with vintage and jewellery shops. ⑫ *Fika Café*, on your right, just past Kensington Place, is a peaceful haven from the action outside. Modelled on Scandinavian cafés, it's airy with a pretty backyard.

End your trip with a bang at ⑬ *El Rey Mezcal Bar*, which serves the Mexican agave spirit that is surging in popularity. Snag a spot on the patio for some taste-testing and people-watching – there's always a cast of colourful characters gathered here.

Getting there

Take the westbound streetcar from Queen's Park Station and alight at Augusta Avenue. Alternatively you can catch the streetcar south from Spadina Station, exit at College Street and walk west to Augusta.

Address book

01 Café Pamenar
307 Augusta Avenue
+1 647 352 3627
cafepamenar.ca

02 Model Citizen
279 Augusta Avenue
+1 416 703 7625
modelcitizentoronto.com

03 Grk Ygrt
291 Augusta Avenue
+1 647 345 0136

04 Good Egg
267 Augusta Avenue
+1 416 593 4663
goodegg.ca

05 Blue Banana Market
250 Augusta Avenue
+1 416 594 6600
bluebananamarket.com

06 Sweet Olenka's
225 Augusta Avenue
+1 647 352 3444
sweetolenkas.ca

07 Bellevue Square Park
5 Bellevue Avenue

08 Kid Icarus
205 Augusta Avenue
+1 416 977 7236
kidicarus.ca

09 Torteria San Cosme
181 Baldwin Street
+1 416 599 2855
sancosme.ca

10 Wilbe Bloomin
160 Baldwin Street
+1 416 597 6222
wilbebloomin.ca

11 Blackbird Baking Co
172 Baldwin Street
+1 416 546 2280
blackbirdbakingco.com

12 Fika Café
28 Kensington Avenue
fika.ca

13 El Rey Mezcal Bar
2A Kensington Avenue
elreybar.com

NEIGHBOURHOOD 03
Leslieville
Eastern promise

Many visitors to Toronto don't venture this far east, making Leslieville one of the city's best-kept secrets. Cut off from the rest of Downtown by the Don River, Leslieville began as the site of the Toronto Nurseries, founded by George Leslie (to whom the area owes its name). It soon grew to become an industrial hub before the decline of the manufacturing sector led to harsh economic times.

The area has been steadily recovering since the 1990s thanks to an influx of young people and families joining longtime residents and businesses. By the 2010s it was buzzing again. It's this mix of new and old that makes Leslieville so special. On your walk along Queen Street East you'll notice shops, restaurants, and cafes sporting a streak of classic Toronto charm yet exuding contemporary appeal. There's also a discerning sense of community in the air. Families walk to the park, dogs and carriages in tow. And for after-hours fun there's a vibrant bar scene.

While Queen Street is often the focal point of Leslieville, its northern side boasts some of Toronto's oldest residential communities. With Riverdale Park just to the west, the neighbourhood is as suited for a casual stroll in nature as it is for a night on the town.

Old and new tour
Leslieville walk

Leslieville is fairly spread out so be prepared to cover some ground. And, as with most things in Leslieville, early risers are rewarded. Arrive promptly at ❶ *Rooster Coffee House* at Broadview and Riverdale to earn your place on the patio that overlooks the park. Its coffee is often cited as among the best in the city.

Continue south down Broadview Avenue until you reach Gerrard Street East. Hang a left and walk three blocks until you come to Logan Avenue, where you'll see ❷ *Saturday Dinette*, a revamped diner specialising in comfort food. Treat yourself to a hearty brunch – the menu features items including buckwheat pancakes and shakshuka.

From the diner, trace back the way you came, turning left on Broadview Avenue to continue down the street. When you hit Queen Street East turn left once more; this is the main stretch of Leslieville. Your first stop here, just

two blocks away, is ❸ *Tiny Record Shop*, Leslieville's best source for new and vintage vinyl. Run by the owner of a music label, the modest name belies its vast selection.

When you can peel your ears away, continue down Queen Street, passing ❹ *Bonjour Brioche*, a patisserie serving fragrant baked goods. We recommend the pain au chocolat to take to ❺ *Jimmie Simpson Park*, just past the shop. Depending on the time of year, the park hosts all sorts of events, from food fairs to music festivals.

Once you're rested, keep on down Queen Street East. Passing Logan Avenue, you'll come across ❻ *Ed's Real Scoop* on the left. Treat yourself to some delicious homemade ice cream (all but compulsory for a walk on a hot day).

A few doors up is ❼ *Bill Hicks Bar*, an unexpected twist on the typical rock bar: it's located in a converted apartment. If you're not quite ready for the hard stuff and it's more caffeine you're after, ❽ *Mercury Espresso Bar* is on the corner of Morse Street.

Farther down on the right, one block from Mercury, check in on the ❾ *Good Neighbour*, a retail outlet selling men's and women's clothing and accessories. Notably, its partnered with the Drake General Store *(see page 50)* to bring its unique style of Canadiana-inspired products to the east end.

Once you're stocked up on Hudson's Bay scarves or have picked out a gift or two, head across and down the street to ❿ *Machine Age Modern*. Though there are many vintage-furniture dealers in Leslieville, few match

the selection and curation here. See what they have in stock; you might find a good deal on a 1957 Lotte lamp, originally made in Ontario by Danish immigrant couple Lotte and Gunnar Bostlund.

Just steps away is ⓫ *Eastside Social*, an oyster bar and seafood restaurant. We recommended you stop for a meal on the back patio enjoyed with a paired wine.

Now that you've been fed, a nice evening stroll is the perfect nightcap to your outing. Head east on Queen Street East until you pass Greenwood Avenue. It's a way farther down but eventually you'll hit ⓬ *Ashbridge Estate* on the left-hand side of the street. It's the earliest known residence in the area and now home to the Ontario Archaeological Society. Built in the regency style popular back in the day (and designed by a former Toronto mayor), the house is a heritage landmark. Then hop on a westbound streetcar and you'll find yourself back in Downtown in a matter of minutes.

Getting there

From Broadview Station take the Broadview streetcar south to Withrow. Alternatively take the Dundas streetcar east from Downtown; exit at Broadview Avenue and walk north. Leslieville isn't as well connected to the metro as other parts of the city but the fun is in walking.

Address book

01 Rooster Coffee House
479 Broadview Avenue
+1 416 995 1530
roostercoffeehouse.com

02 Saturday Dinette
807 Gerrard Street East
+1 416 465 5959
saturdaydinette.com

03 Tiny Record Shop
804 Queen Street East
+1 416 479 4363
tinyrecordshop.com

04 Bonjour Brioche
812 Queen Street East
+1 416 406 1250
bonjourbrioche.com

05 Jimmie Simpson Park
870 Queen Street East

06 Ed's Real Scoop
920 Queen Street East
+1 416 406 2525
edsrealscoop.com

07 Bill Hicks Bar
946 Queen Street East

08 Mercury Espresso Bar
915 Queen Street East
+1 647 435 4779

09 Good Neighbour
935 Queen Street East
+1 647 350 0663
goodnbr.com

10 Machine Age Modern
1000 Queen Street East
+1 416 461 3588
machineagemodern.com

11 Eastside Social
1008 Queen Street East
+1 416 461 5663
eastsidesocial.ca

12 Ashbridge Estate
1444 Queen Street East
+1 416 325 5000
heritagetrust.on.ca

NEIGHBOURHOOD 04
Roncesvalles
Village vibe

It's an odd quirk of Toronto that so many neighbourhoods bill themselves as villages, regardless of historical fact. Roncesvalles – Roncy, for short – at least feels more so than most. This is in large part because its main artery has the air of a village high street; it's almost defiantly local and mostly free of big-name retailers. The area is also partly insulated from Toronto's bustle: south is Lake Ontario and to its west is the forest of High Park, which at 161 hectares is the city's largest green space.

Roncesvalles has a reputation for community spiritedness. When the repertory cinema faced closure, residents stepped in to keep it going. What is now Sorauren Park was once slated to be a garage for rubbish-trucks; instead activists ensured its use as a vibrant open-air community centre. That Roncesvalles is ranked one of the city's most desirable areas has much to do with its residents making it so.

The community has been getting younger and more diversified. Young families are drawn to the well-tended Victorian homes, amenities and quick commute Downtown. Many of these newcomers have opened boutiques and restaurants that are bringing life to some of the area's more neglected corners. When people refer to Toronto's superior liveability, Roncy's the kind of area they're thinking about.

Village tour
Roncesvalles walk

Fuel up amid the white-tiled minimalist decor of ❶ *Reunion Island Coffee Bar* on Roncesvalles Avenue. When you leave, turn right and cross the road to the 100-year-old, Edwardian-inspired ❷ *Revue Cinema (see page 102)*, one of the last of Toronto's grand neighbourhood movie houses. It screens a mix of international, indie and classic films and is run by volunteers.

A few shopfronts to the north, peek into ❸ *Livestock*. You may think you've stumbled into a Tokyo streetwear showroom: designed by industrial designer Lukas Peet, it's destination shopping for sneaker freaks and lifestyle-brand loyalists.

Should you find yourself in an analogue mood, continue up the street to take the sharp right on Dundas Street West (you'll almost be doubling back). ❹ *Tonality Records* is stocked with vinyl that tends toward the indie, post-rock and shoegaze spectrum. Don't miss the museum-like back area packed with vintage audio gear.

Head on down Dundas Street West and look out to the right, near the junction with Howard Park Avenue. The oddly shaped white building with red trim is a former Buddhist temple, now home to the recording studio of celebrated music producer Daniel Lanois (Neil Young made an album here). A bit further down, turn left on Morrow Avenue. Just before the dead end, turn right into the courtyard of the converted warehouses. A huge metal door leads to the ❺ *Olga Korper Gallery*. Korper, a gallerist for more than

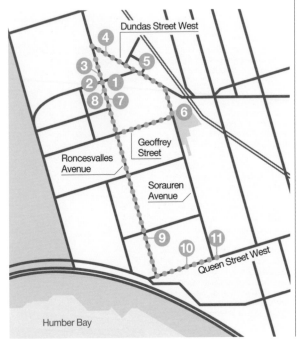

Dundas Street West

Geoffrey Street

Roncesvalles Avenue

Sorauren Avenue

Queen Street West

Humber Bay

40 years, represents an impressive roster of mid to late-career Canadian and international artists.

Back at Dundas Street West, turn left then take the second right down Sorauren Avenue. At ⑥ *Sorauren Park* there's a nice view of the skyline and, on Mondays, a top-notch farmers' market.

Walk up Geoffrey Street, opposite the park. At the end of the street, turn right back onto Roncesvalles Avenue and go a few blocks north to find charming boutique ⑦ *Ardith*, which carries

technical wear and daily basics for women. If you're lucky you'll see the graffiti portrait of the proprietor's grandmother (and the shop's namesake) in the window.

For lunch either grab some Cuban cuisine at ⑧ *La Cubana*, (worth it for the retro-Latino diner design), or turn left and hike several blocks to ⑨ *Sushi Nomi*. With regular shipments from Tokyo's Tsukiji Market, this takeaway shop has some of the city's finest raw fish.

Further south, on the corner of Roncesvalles Avenue and Grafton Avenue, is a massive mural depicting what the waterfront looked like 60 years ago when it was the city's amusement grounds. Today, crossing the bridge to the lake at the foot of Roncesvalles, you'll see parkland and beach. Stroll the boardwalk.

Turn left on Queen Street West and Roncesvalles will begin to blend into the western edges of scruffier Parkdale, home to an unlikely mélange of diasporas. Parkdale's shopping has also improved, with recent arrivals such as ⑩ *North Standard Trading Post*, which carries well-worn US work brands such as Penfield and Red Wing, plus Toronto-designed products and its own-brand casualwear and accessories.

Leaving North Standard, turn left and it's a two-block trot to dinner at ⑪ *Parts and Labour*. Once a hardware store, today it's a large, boisterous room with rows of long communal tables and hanging cylindrical lamps. If there's three or more of you, indulge in one of chef Matty Matheson's satisfying, large-format sharing plates.

Getting there

Roncesvalles is easily accessible at the north end, only a short walk south from the Dundas West subway station. It's also serviced by several intersecting streetcar routes running east-west along Dundas and Queen.

Address book

01 Reunion Island Coffee Bar
385 Roncesvalles Avenue
reunionislandcoffee.com

02 Revue Cinema
400 Roncesvalles Avenue
+1 416 531 9950
revuecinema.ca

03 Livestock
406 Roncesvalles Avenue
+1 647 347 8046
deadstock.ca

04 Tonality Records
2168 Dundas Street West
+1 416 532 8808
tonalityrecords.com

05 Olga Korper Gallery
17 Morrow Avenue
+1 416 538 8220
olgakorpergallery.com

06 Sorauren Park
289 Sorauren Avenue

07 Ardith
373 Roncesvalles Avenue
+1 416 878 7088
ardithstyle.com

08 La Cubana
392 Roncesvalles Avenue
+1 416 538 7500
lacubana.ca

09 Sushi Nomi
67 Roncesvalles Avenue
+1 647 748 7288
sushinomi.com

10 North Standard Trading Post
1662 Queen Street West
+1 647 348 7060
northstandard.com

11 Parts and Labour
1566 Queen Street West
+1 416 588 7750
partsandlabour.ca

NEIGHBOURHOOD 05

Cabbagetown and Corktown
Golden oldies

Cabbagetown and Corktown are next to the deep Rosedale Ravine and the lower Don River area. To visit is to wander into Toronto's past, while stepping right into its rapid east-end revival.

With Victorian-era houses and lush side streets, Cabbagetown makes its case as Toronto's most serene community. Irish immigrants fleeing the Potato Famine in the 19th century planted cabbage on any free land, a practice appalling to the city's established residents, who gave the working-class suburb its name. The 1970s and 1980s saw homebuyers restoring the Georgian, gothic and romanesque homes. Today residents still plant cabbage, give neighbours keys to their homes and host community and garden festivals. City bylaws and heritage protection have helped preserve old Cabbagetown's charm.

Corktown also owes its name to the Irish immigrants who settled here in the 19th century (in this case from County Cork). A few remaining Victorian homes sit next to condos, studios, offices, furniture shops and new restaurants and cafés. Some say Corktown refers to the now-shuttered distilleries, including Gooderham & Worts (which ceased production in 1990 after 153 years in business). Used as a backdrop for hundreds of films, the cobblestone lanes of the Distillery District house some of the city's best shops, galleries and restaurants.

Old-time tour
Cabbagetown and Corktown walk

Start out among the orchids, cacti and date palms under the iron-and-glass canopy (it's more than 100 years old) of the ❶ *Allan Gardens Conservatory*. Then head east on Carlton Street and you'll arrive at ❷ *Labour of Love*, which gets its name from owner Regina Sheung's passion for smart stationery and cards, jewellery and framed silkscreens. Toward the back of the shop you can test handmade lotions from Leaves of Trees and a selection of alcohol bitters from Niagara-based Dillon's Small Batch Distillers.

Continue up Carlton Street and turn right onto Parliament Street. A little way down, secure a patio spot and have brunch at neighbourhood institution ❸ *House on Parliament*. Then head back the way you came. Take a look at the graffiti murals on the corner of Carlton Street and continue up Parliament Street for dairy-free gelato at ❹ *Grinning Face*, prepared by sisters Keo Williamson and

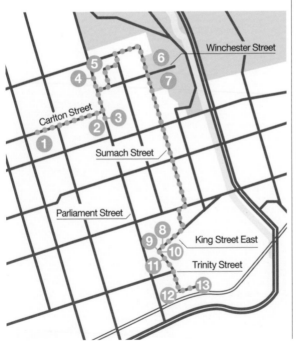

Getting there

Cabbagetown and Corktown can be reached by taking any of the College, Dundas, Queen or King streetcar routes east from the subway stations of the same names along Yonge Street.

Julie Phokeo using a variety of seasonal fruit.

Opposite you might catch Dean Lee making custom light fixtures at ⑤ *Lampcage*. (If you'd like to visit, drop in between 11.00 and 17.00, Tuesday to Saturday.)

Go south to the junction and turn left on Winchester Street; after a block turn left onto Metcalfe Street, a tree-lined strip of preserved Victorian houses. Many homes in the area have heritage plaques, some noting previous owners including Betty Oliphant, co-founder of the National Ballet School. Take a right on Amelia Street and then left, heading to the end of Sackville Street and the Wellesley Cottages, a brick lane of whitewashed workers' homes dating from the late 19th century.

Take the little lane back to Wellesley Street and head east to Sumach Street. On your left as you walk down Sumach Street is Wellesley Park and ⑥ *Toronto Necropolis*. Dating from 1850, it's the resting place of prominent Torontonians such as George Brown (founder of the *Toronto*

Globe) and the city's first mayor, William Lyon Mackenzie. The park hosts a farmers' market in summer. Left on Winchester Street will take you to ⑦ *Riverdale Farm*, which occupies the site of a zoo that relocated to Scarborough in 1974. Enjoy the park before wandering south on Sumach Street. After about 300 metres turn into Regent Park on your right, noting Regent Park Aquatic Centre, designed by Toronto-based firm MacLennan Jaunkalns Miller Architects. Then head back to Sumach and amble south, then right on Queen Street East. Take a left turn on Bright Street. The restored Victorian row-houses lean curiously at the bend of this charming crooked road.

Turn right on King Street East via the mural-adorned underpass and enter ⑧ *Made Design*, where Shaun Moore displays furniture and homeware by as many as 80 independent Canadian designers.

A few doors down, in one of the best-preserved brick buildings in the area, is ⑨ *Tandem Coffee*. Grab an espresso or wander a couple of doors up to ⑩ *Roselle Desserts* and enjoy a pastry at the bright, cosy French-inspired bakery. Right opposite is Trinity Street and ⑪ *Enoch Turner Schoolhouse*, the museum on the site of the city's first free public school, dating to 1848.

Pass on to Mill Street and the ⑫ *Distillery District*, with its many shops, galleries, cafés and restaurants in the old warehouse (once owned and used by Gooderham & Worts, one of Canada's largest distillers). Catch a show at ⑬ *The Young Centre for the Performing Arts*, and after you're done, hail a cab on Mill Street.

Address book

01 Allan Gardens Conservatory
   19 Horticultural Avenue
   +1 416 392 7288
   torontobotanicalgarden.ca

02 Labour of Love
   223 Carlton Street
   +1 416 923 8988
   thelabouroflove.ca

03 House on Parliament
   454 Parliament Street
   +1 416 925 4074
   houseonparliament.com

04 Grinning Face
   540 Parliament Street
   +1 416 920 4444
   grinningface.ca

05 Lampcage
   557 Parliament Street
   +1 416 686 5350
   lampcage.com

06 Toronto Necropolis
   200 Winchester Street
   +1 416 923 7911

07 Riverdale Farm
   201 Winchester Street
   +1 416 362 6794

08 Made Design
   394 King Street East
   +1 416 607 6384
   madedesign.ca

09 Tandem Coffee
   368 King Street East
   tandemcoffee.ca

10 Roselle Desserts
   362 King Street East
   +1 416 368 8188
   roselleto.com

11 Enoch Turner Schoolhouse
   106 Trinity Street
   +1 416 327 6997
   enochturnerschoolhouse.ca

12 Distillery District
   55 Mill Street
   +1 416 364 1177
   thedistillerydistrict.com

13 The Young Centre for the Performing Arts
   50 Tank House Lane
   +1 416 866 8666
   youngcentre.ca

Resources
—— Inside knowledge

Laid out on a grid, Toronto is a simple enough city to navigate. That said, finding the easiest route from A to B can be tricky – and often involves switching from train to bus to streetcar. Sometimes getting around by bike is the best option. Whatever you choose, we've listed the information you need to find your way.

In a city of many ethnicities it's not so much your accent that exposes you as an outsider but the words you choose. We've added a mini glossary of Torontonian language quirks so you can sound like you belong.

And while you will have no shortage of things to see and do, we've thrown in some extra suggestions for making the most of the city come rain or shine. Our event listing will keep you up to date with annual must-sees. And finally, we've rounded up some favourite songs to provide a soundtrack to your explorations.

Transport
Get around town

01 Toronto Transit Commission: The TTC runs the city's network of subways, streetcars and buses. It costs CA$3.25 for a single journey if you pay by cash, CA$2.90 with a Presto card (see below) and CA$12 for a day pass.
ttc.ca

02 Presto card: After relying on metallic tokens for more than half a century, Torontonians are switching to the Presto card. The tap-and-pay system works on the subway, Go Trains and Union Pearson Express.
prestocard.ca

03 Airports: Toronto Pearson International Airport lies 26.5km northwest of Downtown and is the main international hub. Billy Bishop Airport on Toronto Island (accessed from the mainland via a six-minute walk through a tunnel) is used by both international and national carriers (Porter Airlines offers multiple daily flights from here to nearby cities such as Montréal, New York and Chicago).
torontopearson.com; portstoronto.com

04 Union Pearson Express: This service is the quickest way to get to Downtown from Toronto Pearson International Airport. The journey takes about 25 minutes and costs CA$12, with trains departing every 15 minutes.
upexpress.com

05 Cycling: While Downtown's heavy traffic can be intimidating for cyclists, residential areas are very bike-friendly. There are more than 200 Bike Share Toronto hire stations throughout the city and well-marked cycle lanes. A day pass costs CA$7.
bikesharetoronto.com

06 Taxi: There is rarely a shortage of taxis and ride-share apps are also commonly used.

Vocabulary
Local lingo

This nifty list of terms will have you sounding like a Torontonian in no time.

01 Eh: most Canadians punctuate their questions with this clipped syllable: "What do you think, eh?"
02 T'rono: no native would be caught dead enunciating the second "t"
03 Touque: a beanie (hat)
04 Double-double: coffee with two creams and two sugars
05 Kerfuffle: an altercation, particularly one that occurs during a hockey match
06 Canuck: a Canadian

Toronto playlist
Now hear this

01 Drake, 'Know Yourself': This hip-hop tune from Toronto's biggest music export is from his 2015 album *If You're Reading This it's too Late*.
02 Bart, 'On/Off': Singers Christopher Shannon and Nathan Vanderwielen's emotive falsettos, clean guitar riffs and soulful saxophone are only the tip of this iceberg. The rest of their album *Holomew* is equally memorable.
03 Diana, 'Born Again': This psychedelic track makes for a compelling introduction to home-grown synthpop band Diana's inaugural album *Perpetual Surrender*.
04 Vallens, 'Dark Tunnel': This beautifully immersive song from singer Robyn Phillips takes listeners on a journey down an auditory rabbit hole.
05 Daniel Romano, 'Valerie Leon': An homage to the English actress, Romano's playful tune throws back to the 1960s. His nasal baritone is accompanied by fast strings and beats.

Best events
What to see

01 Interior Design Show, Entertainment District: Preview the latest in design by national and global talent. *January, interiordesign show.com*

02 Hot Docs, Mirvish Village: More than 200 international and domestic films are screened at North America's biggest documentary festival. *April to May, hotdocs.ca*

03 Luminato, citywide: This arts-and-design festival brings with it installations, concerts and exhibitions. *June, luminatofestival.com*

04 NXNE, citywide: Toronto's answer to SXSW in Austin, this music festival hosts the world's best indie acts. *June, nxne.com*

05 Pride Month, Church-Wellesley Village: This annual affair culminates in a parade that celebrates the city's progressive values. *June to July, pridetoronto.com*

06 Toronto International Film Festival, Entertainment District: This festival in the Tiff Bell Lightbox (*see page 101*) is an avenue to preview possible Oscar contenders. *September, tiff.net*

07 Nuit Blanche, citywide: For one night residents transform the streets with art installations and more. *October, nbto.com*

08 International Festival of Authors, Harbourfront Centre: This literary event is an opportunity to hear from writers across all genres. *October, ifoa.org*

09 Christmas Market, Distillery District: Come Christmas, this red-bricked district transforms into a European-style market. *November to December, torontochristmasmarket.com*

10 Trampoline Hall, venue varies: A regular roving lecture series for Toronto's intellectuals. *Monthly, trampolinehall.net*

Rainy days
Weather-proof activities

The indoor activities below aren't only great options when it rains: they'll come in handy during the winter months too.

01 Ryerson Image Centre, Garden District: Conveniently located in the heart of the shopping district, the Ryerson Image Centre may be a research centre for photography but it also hosts numerous cutting-edge exhibitions that draw in the crowds. *ryerson.ca/ric*

02 Catch a live taping of 'Rick Mercer Report', Entertainment District: Free tickets are available online to many live talk shows recorded at the CBC headquarters, including the satirical *Rick Mercer Report*. Be sure to apply well in advance because tickets get snapped up. *rickmercer.com*

03 Roberts Gallery, Yorkville: Avail yourself of a comprehensive survey of Canadian fine art at the Roberts Gallery, just a nudge south of Bloor Street on Yonge Street. Originally founded in 1842, the showroom has passed through three families and today deals exclusively with Canadian art, both historical and contemporary. *robertsgallery.net*

04 Learn to somersault at the Toronto School of Circus Arts, Downsview Park: Don't let inclement weather deter you from doing some physical activity. The Toronto School of Circus Arts conducts drop-in trapeze classes every Friday. *torontocircus.com*

Sunny days
The great outdoors

Toronto comes alive in the summer when it's warm enough to spend time outdoors. Here's how to make the most of it.

01 Explore the city's indigenous history: The Native Canadian Centre of Toronto has launched the *First Story* app that serves as an alternative mobile guide to the city. Create your own walk and learn about the city's indigenous cultures. *ncct.on.ca*

02 Yard sales: Queen West, Dundas West, College and Bloor West streets are bustling shopping strips that run parallel to each other. On the weekend, however, a more casual form of commerce takes place between them at ad hoc yard sales. Wander through the eclectic mix of residential blocks and you're bound to chance upon a hidden gem.

03 Little Italy audio tour: If you're visiting Little Italy you may want to download an audio tour called *The Slow Now*. It starts at the northwest corner of College and Manning and is a poetic portrait of the area. When you're done, drop by The Monocle Shop and say hi. *koffler.digital/theslownow*

04 Toronto Botanical Garden: It may be out of the way but this area of greenery is the perfect escape from the concrete jungle of Downtown core. *torontobotanicalgarden.ca*

05 Take a day trip to Prince Edward County: A three-hour drive east will bring you to a wine region with few tourists. The sand dunes of Sandbanks Provincial Park are worth a stop, as is a meal at Drake Devonshire, a waterfront inn by the folks behind The Drake Hotel (*see page 23*). *drakedevonshire.ca*

About Monocle
—— Step inside

In 2007 Monocle was launched as a monthly magazine briefing on global affairs, business, culture, design and much more. We believed there was a globally minded audience of readers who were hungry for opportunities and experiences beyond their national borders.

Today Monocle is a complete media brand with print, audio and online elements – not to mention our expanding network of shops and cafés. Besides our London HQ we have seven international bureaux in New York, Toronto, Istanbul, Singapore, Tokyo, Zürich and Hong Kong. We continue to grow and flourish and at our core is the simple belief that there will always be a place for a print brand that is committed to telling fresh stories and sending photographers on assignments. It's also a case of knowing that our success is all down to the readers, advertisers and collaborators who have supported us along the way.

❶
Retail and cafés
Food for thought

Via our shops in Toronto, Hong Kong, New York, Tokyo, London and Singapore we sell products that cater to our readers' tastes and are produced in collaboration with brands we believe in. We also have cafés in Tokyo and London. And if you are in the UK capital, visit the Kioskafé in Paddington, which combines good coffee and great reads.

❷
International bureaux
Boots on the ground

We have an HQ in London and call upon firsthand reports from our correspondents in more than 35 cities around the world. We also have seven international bureaux; for this travel guide Toronto bureau chief Tomos Lewis and deputy bureau chief Jason Li used their expertise to showcase the best of Toronto. They also called on the assistance of writers and researchers in the city to ensure that we covered the best food, retail, hospitality and entertainment on offer. The aim is to make you, the reader, feel like a local when you visit.

❸
Online
Digital delivery

We have a dynamic website: *monocle.com*. As well as being the place to hear our radio station, Monocle 24, the site presents our films, which are beautifully shot and edited by our in-house team and provide a fresh perspective on our stories. Check out the films celebrating the cities that make up our Travel Guide Series before you explore the rest of the site.

 Radio
Sound approach

Monocle 24 is our round-the-clock radio station that was launched in 2011. It delivers global news and shows covering foreign affairs, urbanism, business, culture, food and drink, design and print media. When you find yourself in Toronto, tune into *The Daily* to hear regular reports from our Toronto and New York bureaus and interviews with guests from across the Americas region. We also have a playlist to accompany you day and night, regularly assisted by live band sessions that are hosted at our headquarters. You can listen to our shows live or download them from *monocle.com*, iTunes or SoundCloud.

5 Print
Committed to the page

MONOCLE is published 10 times a year. We have stayed loyal to our belief in quality print with two extra seasonal publications: THE FORECAST, packed with key insights into the year ahead, and THE ESCAPIST, our summer travel-minded magazine. To sign up visit *monocle.com/subscribe*. Since 2013 we have also been publishing books, like this one, in partnership with Gestalten.

Priority service
—
Subscribers save 10 per cent online

Join the club

01
Subscribe to Monocle
A subscription is a simple way to make sure you never miss a copy and enjoy many additional benefits.

02
Read every issue published
Our subscribers have exclusive access to the entire Monocle archive and have priority access to selected product collaborations at *monocle.com*.

03
Never miss an issue
Subscription copies are delivered to your door no matter where you are in the world and we offer an auto-renewal service to ensure that you never miss an issue.

04
And there's more...
Subscribers benefit from a 10 per cent discount at all Monocle shops, including online, and receive exclusive offers and invitations to events around the world. *monocle.com/subscribe*

Choose your package

Premium one year
12 × issues
+ Porter Sub Club bag
—
One year
12 × issues
+ Monocle Voyage tote bag
—
Six months
6 × issues

Chief photographer
Lorne Bridgman

Still life
David Sykes

Images
Jerry Abramowicz
AGO
Abbas Akhavan
Tom Arban
Leila Ashtray
Titus Chan
Philip Cheung
Jacknife Design
Dylan + Jeni
Geoffrey Farmer
Joel Gale
Shai Gil
Dave Gillespie
Lucia Graca
Michael Graydon & Nikole Herriot
Alexis Hobbs
Jaime Hogge
Chris Hutcheson
Sam Javanrouh
Richard Johnson
Lisa Kannakko
Dimitri Karakostas
Janet Kimber
Lauren Koly
Lauren Kolyn
Isabella Le Marchant Romano
Emma McIntyre
Arash Moallemi
Gary Otte
Vik Pahwa
Ben Rahn
Jonathan Root
Stuart Sakai
Volker Seding
Guillaume Simoneau
Jessica Blaine Smith
Drake General Store
Ryan Thompson
Bruce Zinger

Illustrators
Satoshi Hashimoto
Ceylan Sahin
Tokuma

Writers
Daniel Bach
Cameron Bailey
Marilyn Bell DiLascio
Alex Bozikovic
Dani Couture
Ben Craik
Michael Di Leo
Tim Draimin
Aaron Fox
Christopher Frey
Sarah Fulford
Avery Guerin
Noor Ibrahim
Tomos Lewis
Jason Li
Karen MacKenna
Jennifer Pagliaro
Denise Pinto
Jeremy Schipper
Jake Tobin Garrett
John Tory
Kerala Woods

Monocle

EDITOR IN CHIEF AND CHAIRMAN
Tyler Brûlé
EDITOR
Andrew Tuck
CREATIVE DIRECTOR
Richard Spencer Powell

The Monocle Travel Guide: Toronto
GUIDE EDITORS
Tomos Lewis
Jason Li
PHOTO EDITOR
Faye Sakura Rentoule

The Monocle Travel Guide Series
SERIES EDITOR
Joe Pickard
ASSOCIATE EDITOR, BOOKS
Amy Richardson
RESEARCHER/WRITER
Mikaela Aitken
DESIGNERS
Jay Yeo
Sam Brogan
PHOTO EDITORS
Matthew Beaman
Faye Sakura Rentoule
Shin Miura

PRODUCTION
Jacqueline Deacon
Dan Poole
Chloë Ashby
Sean McGeady
Sonia Zhuravlyova

CHAPTER EDITING

Need to know
Tomos Lewis

Hotels
Jason Li
Tomos Lewis

Food and Drink
Tomos Lewis

Retail
Jason Li

Things we'd buy
Tomos Lewis
Jason Li

Essays
Tomos Lewis

Culture
Tomos Lewis

Design and architecture
Jason Li

Sport and fitness
Tomos Lewis

Walks
Jason Li

Resources
Jason Li

Research
Mikaela Aitken
Beatrice Carmi
Clarissa Pharr
Melanie Tam
Aliz Tennant
Kerala Woods
Zayana Zulkiflee

Special thanks
Maxine Bailey
Jessica Chen
Vince Di Carlo
Jodi DiLascio
Zahra Ebrahim
Megan Gibson
Elly Green
Heather Kelley
Pete Kempshall
Braden Labonte
Christopher Lacroix
Edward Lawrenson
Juan Carlos Leal
Christina Pretti
Jordan Puopol
Roland Rom Colthoff
Mar Sellars
Angela Shackel
Elli Stühler
Gaëtane Verna
Loi Xuan Ly
Rita Zekas

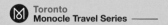

New

The MONOCLE Travel Guide Series 15 Ⓜ
Copenhagen

The MONOCLE Travel Guide Series 16 Ⓜ
Los Angeles

Ⓜ
Buy today at all good bookshops

——

Or visit the online shops at
monocle.com and
shop.gestalten.com

The collection

We hope you have found the Monocle Travel Guide to Toronto useful, inspiring and entertaining. There's plenty more to get your teeth into: we have a global suite of guides, with many more set to be released in coming months. Cities are fun. Let's explore.

❶ London
The sights, sounds and style

❷ New York
Get a taste of the Big Apple's best

❸ Tokyo
The enigmatic glory of Japan's capital

❹ Hong Kong
Down to business in this vibrant city

❺ Madrid
Captivating capital abuzz with spirit

❻ Bangkok
Stimulate your senses with the exotic

❼ Istanbul
Thrilling fusion of Asia and Europe

❽ Miami
Unpack the Magic City's box of tricks

❾ Rio de Janeiro
Beaches, bars and bossa nova

❿ Paris
Be romanced by the City of Light

⓫ Singapore
Where modernity meets tradition

⓬ Vienna
Waltz through the Austrian capital

⓭ Sydney
Sun, surf and urban delights

⓮ Honolulu
Embrace Hawaii's aloha spirit

⓯ Copenhagen
Cycle through the Danish capital

⓰ Los Angeles
Fly high in the City of Angels

⓱ Toronto
Delve into this diverse Canadian city